Sherlock Holmes
WHODUNITS

Sherlock Holmes

WHODUNITS

Can you crack the case?

JOEL JESSUP

SIRIUS

SIRIUS

This edition published in 2024 by Sirius Publishing, a division of
Arcturus Publishing Limited,
26/27 Bickels Yard, 151–153 Bermondsey Street,
London SE1 3HA

ISBN: 978-1-3988-4346-2
AD011985NT

Printed in China

Contents

Introduction

Mrs. Grabber's bed and breakfast had been difficult to find, as the local residents were strangely guarded about its location, but we found our way there, nonetheless. It was a small, innocuous old house, and the door was answered by a small, innocuous lady.

"Madam, my name is Dr. John Watson." I said.

"I know," she replied with irritation, before showing surprise at the identity of my companion: Detective Stanley Hopkins of Scotland Yard!

That morning I had received a summons to meet at Paddington Station, signed SH. I assumed it was from my friend Sherlock Holmes, but it was a welcome surprise to see Detective Hopkins there, as he had assisted us on several cases. He looked uneasy as he explained our destination, saying that Holmes had asked him not to explain anything until we arrived.

We got a carriage from Bodmin Road Station to the small hamlet of Trenale and from there to Mrs Grabber's house, as Holmes' message to Hopkins had indicated. He was sitting at her kitchen table with a broad smile.

"Glad to see you found the place," he said teasingly.

"What's all this about, Holmes?"

"Crimes, Watson. Theft and murder and wickedness of every stripe."

I peered at the sour-faced Mrs. Grabber, who didn't look like a mastermind.

"Just get on with it," she snapped. "I don't want you disrupting my guests."

"You have never had guests," Holmes said lightly. He showed Hopkins a small folder, marked with a large black A.

"That's the file," said Hopkins.

"Last night at 2am, I asked Detective Hopkins to take this police file about Moriarty's deck of cards and stamp it with the letter A." said Holmes. "He left it unattended, and at 5 am someone dressed as a cleaner took the file from the police station, unaware that I was following them. The file changed hands several times, always between servants or

other low-status workers, one of whom then took a train and carriage to this destination. I followed them as they laid the file at Mrs Grabber's door and then took the opportunity to present it personally..."

"But why?" I asked.

"Have you heard of the Anathema Archive?" he asked. I shook my head.

"I have often heard policemen speak of it, but shamefully dismissed it as superstition." He continued. "Recent events made me realize that it might actually exist."

"But what is it?" I asked.

"Follow me," he replied, and he led us out of the kitchen and to a cupboard door that opened to a cold, dark tunnel. We descended until we reached a heavy wooden door, which Mrs. Grabber reluctantly opened with an enormous iron key. Inside were hundreds upon hundreds of files piled and lined up on rows of shelves. It was difficult to see how large the room was as light was provided by an oil lamp on a table, but it was considerable.

"This is the Anathema Archive. The final resting place for any case that the police want to forget...forever."

Holmes picked up a decaying parchment.

"Whenever any member of any police force in Britain has an unsolved case that they simply don't want to exist, they mark it with a large black A and leave it unattended. A member of a secret network spirits it away."

I was baffled. "Why?"

"Some cases can put vulnerable people in danger," said Hopkins.

"Or embarrass powerful people," added Holmes.

"Sometimes a case seems so strange we worry it would frighten the public," said Hopkins.

"Or titillate the press," said Holmes.

"No, what I mean is, why not simply burn the file? Tear it up?" I asked.

"Files sent to the Archive are stricken from the record and forbidden to be spoken about again." said Holmes.

"Who's in charge? Who oversees the theft of the files?" I asked.

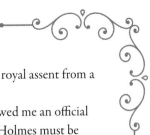

"We're not thieves!" said Mrs. Grabber loudly. "We have permanent royal assent from a higher power."

"The higher power that granted me this writ?" said Holmes. He showed me an official document, signed by the Prime Minister, that demanded that Sherlock Holmes must be granted immediate access to the Anathema Archive with no interference.

"I waved that document at Inspector Lestrade, and he told me I was welcome to peruse the Archives if I could find them, so I recruited Detective Hopkins."

"The Archive is not just a way to cover things up," said Hopkins, defensively. "A policeman often marks a document when they think solving the case is impossible!"

"It is my stock-in-trade to untangle the seemingly impossible. And with modern scientific techniques, we will solve every single case in the Anathema Archive!"

Of course, at this time I didn't know the true reason why Holmes felt he had to solve every case in the archive. I didn't know that a man's life, and perhaps the fate of the whole world, hung in the balance. And time was running out…

Level One Cases

1 The Fading Photograph

Maria Lambert was a success in Surrey's music hall in the 1860s. According to the Anathema Archive, she was involved in a minor scandal in 1869 with a German royal and a disappearing photograph!

The file had been sent by the now deceased Sergeant Eldridge, so we journeyed to Guildford by train to meet the other officer involved, Sergeant Jack Canning.

"Miss Lambert said she'd had a blackmail letter," he said. "Compromising daguerreotypes taken by some German prince who'd visited: Karl Alexander, Duke of Gottschalk. The blackmailer asked for 500 bob! Miss Lambert was a legend, but she didn't have that much."

"So, you suggested setting a trap," replied Holmes.

"Yes, catch the blackmailer during the exchange. Luckily Sergeant Eldridge liked the idea. We arranged for it to happen at the corn exchange. The sergeant, Constable Taft, and I covered the exits. Miss Lambert entered with the bag of 'money,' and we watched. Suddenly Katharine Aykroyd appears and starts screaming at Miss Lambert!"

"A local woman?" I asked.

"Yes, apparently, she'd made her a few dresses. Claimed she was owed money. I thought she was going to hit her, so I intervened, but as I grabbed her, suddenly the bag was gone!"

"You saw no one?"

"Maybe a quick, dark shape, but suddenly I noticed this envelope on the table. I picked it up and someone had forgotten to seal it, so a photo slipped out, and, well... it's not right for me to comment. But it was her alright... I won't elaborate."

"Yes, Sergeant Eldridge reports that you and Miss Lambert looked at the photo in horror," said Holmes.

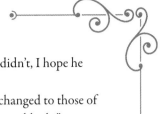

"But he didn't see it himself, right?" asked Canning. "He swore he didn't, I hope he wasn't lying."

"Not initially," said Holmes. "But then he reported that your cries changed to those of confusion, and he couldn't resist looking... only to see that the picture was blank!"

Eldridge looked shaken by the memory.

"That's right! It faded out entirely until it was blank white. Almost like... the man upstairs had stepped in to protect Miss Lambert. Well, after writing it all up Eldridge told me he had to put the case in the vault. I don't mind talking about it now as Miss Lambert passed away about five years ago. No idea what happened to the photo."

But Holmes and I knew, as he had shown it to me back in London, after he had tested the paper with a brace of chemical solutions. It did indeed look like a totally blank piece of albumin paper.

"I would swear that no image has ever been on this paper," said Holmes with irritation. "There should be some kind of faded remainder, a ghost. But there is nothing."

Before we left to visit Miss Aykroyd, Holmes entered a nearby police station and asked to use their telephone to call Germany.

The baffled policemen watched as Holmes conducted a swift conversation in German before hanging up sharply.

"Either Karl Alexander is an incredible liar, or he has never met Miss Lambert."

"Could his advanced years have caused his memory to fade, like the picture?" I asked.

"No, he's sharp as a pickelhaube. But the line was rather poor."

Miss Aykroyd was now Mrs. Hunt, and we found her to be a cheery, matronly lady, living in a warren-like house filled with doilies and grandchildren. But the edges that family life may have worn away re-emerged when we mentioned Miss Lambert, her beaming smile becoming a frown.

"I'd always make her dresses, and then she'd quibble about every detail to get my price down!"

"Yet you continued to work for her?" asked Holmes.

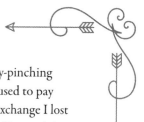

"Well, how often do you get to work for a real performer, even a penny-pinching has-been?" Mrs. Hunt said, lowering her voice. "But on that day, she'd refused to pay for a beautiful gown I'd slaved weeks to make, and when I saw her at the exchange I lost my temper. I had no idea what was going on! But when I saw that photo of her and that German man... Shocking stuff."

"And then it faded?" asked Holmes.

"...Yes! Very strange. But then, her career faded long before the photo did! No scandal would change that, especially in Surrey. We liked our singers to be nice women."

Her expression became more guarded after this, and she returned to matronly mode, but Holmes had no more questions, and we left the house.

"Did the blackmailer hope Miss Lambert would get the money from the duke?" I asked. "But how did the photo fade?"

"A picture can be worth more than many words. Or vice versa," said Holmes.

Question: Who was responsible for the attempted blackmail of Miss Lambert?

Hint: Witnesses.

2 The Premature Ghost

"Do you think you can see a man's ghost before his death?" said Holmes as we entered a market in Maidstone, Kent.

"Holmes, you know ghosts do not exist," I responded.

Fifteen years earlier, Edward Going was found fatally stabbed in an alleyway near this market. A local thug, he had many enemies. It was declared a simple robbery, but 10 minutes earlier three women, all associated with Going, had seen his "ghost" standing on the street about 200 yards from where he was found.

"We saw straight through him!" said Georgie Bidler. She owned a grocery stall in the market. "I knew it was him as he was wearing that brooch. Then I heard he was still alive when they found him! He died soon after, but we were all confused."

"You hated him?" Holmes asked.

"I thought he'd change after marriage," she said. "Then I found out he was already married! He had this brooch he kept locks of hair in; he asked for mine, but I saw there was already hair inside. I said he was unfaithful. But he just laughed and said I'd still marry him anyway. I left soon after. Then I met Mary and Emma."

She waved to the two women currently tending to the stall.

"...That's his wife and... the other lady?" I asked.

"Yes. We moved in together. He was angry, started following us around. Saying the brooch was to remember us by, like he was going to kill us..."

The brooch was missing from Going when he was found, ripped from the left side of his chest.

"But his ghost was wearing the brooch? On which side?" asked Holmes.

"On the right. I did think it was strange, as he always said he would keep our locks close to his heart."

We next spoke to Mary, his former wife. In contrast to Georgie, she was much more timid, looking ashamed of the whole enterprise.

"Edward was not such a bad man when we met. When I saw the vision..."

"The 'ghost?'" I added.

"You cannot see a ghost before someone's died. I understand now it was a vision of what was to come," she said with total confidence.

"Do you think the other ladies could have killed him?" asked Holmes.

Mary was offended by this. "No! they may seem rough, but they have good hearts. They would never take a life!"

"After the... vision, did you all remain together?" I asked.

Mary frowned in concentration. "No. When I saw him like that, with the brooch over his heart as usual, I felt faint. Georgie went to fetch water and Emma to find the constable. The next thing I hear is that they've found him stabbed!"

Emma Wainwright would be described as "strapping" by most measures and seemed indifferent.

"I don't see the point in going over this. That worm had so many enemies. Only good thing he ever did for me was give me the chance to meet Georgie and Mary. So, when I saw his ghost I wasn't frightened, I've seen ghosts before. I was pleased."

"But he hadn't died at that point," said Holmes.

"I don't know about that, I wasn't there when they found him; maybe they just thought he was alive. My uncle was an undertaker; he said bodies do all sorts of odd things after they've died."

"Was he wearing his brooch?" Holmes asked.

"Can't say I noticed, I was looking at his expression, he looked surprised. Suppose I would if I had been stabbed."

Holmes established where they had seen the ghost and convinced them to take us there when the day's work was done. It was on a short street lined with shops and a few residences. Holmes went to stand on the spot where they had seen the apparition and peered up at the shop's signage.

Pepper's Ghost

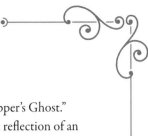

"A glazier. I thought so. Was this here 15 years ago?"

They all nodded to the affirmative.

"Then what happened is clear. It was an accidental illusion called Pepper's Ghost."

As Holmes explained, a piece of glass angled correctly can produce a reflection of an unseen figure, seemingly transparent and disconnected.

"Going was trying to hide from you, but the glaziers had no doubt placed a sheet of glass here that revealed him to you. A simple trick. But one that has also revealed to me which of you murdered him..."

Question: Who does Sherlock Holmes suspect murdered Edward Going?

Hint: Brooch.

3   The Tell-Tale Tureen

Twenty-five years ago, the Larthrabore family, living in a mansion near King's Lynn, were robbed of silver platters, cutlery, and serving dishes that had been in their possession for centuries. The staff fell under suspicion but there was no evidence, save a single tureen discovered in a sack in a barn a mile away.

"Fingerprints can remain indefinitely, depending on how and where the object is kept," Holmes said as he examined the tureen. He found three clear sets. They matched with three people still employed by the family:

- Elsie Dent, formerly the under cook, now cook.
- Millie Orwell, formerly kitchen maid, now under cook.
- And Sissy Blight, formerly scullery maid and now lady's maid to Lady Larthrabore.

All three worked in the kitchen and the tureen was used the day before the theft, so it would have been more unusual if it didn't bear their fingerprints!
Elsie was a cheery woman with a naturally rosy complexion.

"We had the Greenacres come round, and the previous Lady Larthrabore wanted me to make a pear tart that Lord Greenacre enjoyed. I was arm deep in flour when the tureen was retrieved. It was a cold day, colder even than today, so the dough was stiff. I had my hands on the tureen for a second, getting it to Miss Blight so she could help Millie get the consommé in it and take it to the table."

"There are no traces of flour," Holmes remarked.

"After 30 years?" she said. "It's possible I washed my hands before I touched it."

"Your father had gambling debts..." Holmes remarked.

"I didn't have anything to do with him," she replied. "In the end he went to Ireland. I hadn't seen him for years by the time of the robbery. Mrs. Blight needed money; she had expensive tastes for a scullery maid!"

Millie Orwell was a prim woman with a neutral expression.

"It was cold for August! An omen for the robbery? Though it must have happened in the night, and the next day was warm, forgive my superstition."

"Do think Mrs. Dent or Mrs. Blight may have taken the items?" I asked her.

She leaned forward.

"If you want a suspect, there was a young man from the village who was always hanging around. I think he was interested in Elsie, but she was either oblivious or knew better than to associate with him. He stopped coming round after the robbery! I told the police, but they didn't seem to care."

"Did you have any resentment toward the family?" Holmes said.

"No. Do you think I would remain here if I did? I've worked here for 36 years!" she declaimed.

"Not even after your accident?" he said.

Mrs. Orwell peered down at her foot, which I could now see was twisted round unnaturally.

"Mr. Holmes, I never blamed them for what happened; no one could have predicted that the horse would kick like that. And they were very kind to me afterward. I've never been treated poorly by the Larthrabores."

Sissy Blight seemed slightly offended that we needed to speak to her about that day, wringing her gloved hands in agitation.

"The family were so upset by it. I feel Lady Larthrabore, that is, the previous Lady Larthrabore, never truly recovered from the loss. When they found the tureen, we hoped it might have been a glimmer of light, but when it did not lead to anything it became a sort of taunting relic of what had been, and she insisted it be locked away forever."

"You were helping in the kitchen that day?" asked Holmes.

"Yes, I had only just returned from the village as we didn't have enough pears for the tart, and I had barely got through the door when the tureen was thrust into my hands! I did not usually assist with the cooking. Mrs. Dent always said I was clumsy because of my condition, just because the cold affects me so badly. I dropped one plate once and that was it, it didn't even have anything to do with my condition!"

"Were you having any problems with money at this time?" asked Holmes.

"You mean like Elsie and Millie? Not at all, I've always been sensible," she said, crossing her arms. "If you ask me, one of them left the back door open by accident and some opportunist took the chance to steal everything. Or maybe they did it deliberately and he left the tureen as a thank you gift."

Once we were alone, I shook my head that three people could so casually incriminate each other after over 30 years of working together. "Shame that the fingerprints couldn't really tell us anything," I remarked.

"On the contrary, the fingerprints told us everything!" declared Holmes.

Question: Who does Sherlock Holmes suspect robbed the Larthrabores?

Hint: The cold.

4 The Blasted Stump

Four years ago, the village of Ferndene in Cumbria had been plagued by poison pen letters revealing the resident's secrets, threatening exposure if they didn't leave money at "the lightning tree."

"It was actually a stump on the edge of the village split by lightning decades ago," said Constable Renfrew. "A few victims approached me as they couldn't pay. I planned a trap, got one of them, the postmaster Mr. Patton, to drop some money off at the stump. I watched the whole time as he walked there, left the bag and walked back, and we waited. After two hours, nothing. The sun began to set so I went to get the bag… and it was empty!"

"Could Mr. Patton have pocketed the money?" I asked as the Constable walked us to the location of the stump.

In the intervening years Patton had been found guilty of a different crime, as had Brenda Wakefield and the town's former vicar, Reverend Peter Livingstone.

"I checked the bag myself before he left. And I watched him walk the whole way! Even though it was a little misty, I could easily make his postman's uniform out..."

He showed us the small shed where he and Patton had observed the stump. As he pointed it out in the distance he was confused.

"That's odd..."

We saw not one, but two blackened stumps in the distance.

"Which was it?" asked Holmes.

"...The right one. The left was not there before; it was a tall tree! I remember Mr. Patton passing behind it for a moment. Must have been struck by lightning since then!"

"Was anyone else in the area?"

"No. The barmaid was seen in the woods the night before. But at that time, nobody."

Holmes inspected both stumps confirming they were solid, save for the small hollow in the right one. Crouching by the left-hand stump he picked up a small handful of something.

"Pipe tobacco," he remarked.

The Postmaster, Mr. Clifford Patton, served his time for stealing mail, and now worked as a hired hand.

"The money I lost paying off the blackmailer meant I had to take the postal orders!" he declared.

"You volunteered to help Constable Renfrew catch him?" asked Holmes.

"He asked me. I was considered trustworthy until the bad business. I was the only postman. I asked for another; they just sent an extra uniform."

"Was anyone else near the stump?" said Holmes.

"Thought I saw that vicar, but in that mist it could have been a deer."

"Who did you suspect?" I asked.

"That eavesdropping barmaid!" he declared.

"Do you smoke, Mr. Patton?" Holmes asked.

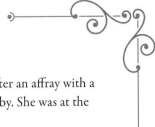

"No, I save my money for ale," he said.

Mrs. Wakefield was dismissed from her role in the village's pub after an affray with a customer but had been hired in roughly the same role in a town nearby. She was at the bar, which was carved into some medieval design.

"Customer gave me lip, so I bopped him on the head," she said. "Landlord didn't like it, so I left."

"What information were you being blackmailed with, if you don't mind?" asked Holmes.

"I do mind, and none of your business!" she retorted. "But I wasn't in support of paying. If you do, it never stops."

"How long did it take you to carve this?" asked Holmes, indicating the bar's design.

"How did you...?" she started. "Wait, you probably spotted bits of wood under my nails, or my hand has rough skin from holding a chisel..."

"You've carved BW into the corner here," Holmes said, pointing. "My only other question is, do you smoke a pipe?"

"Is that a joke? I can't stand them. That's why I bopped Mansley; he was puffing it right in my face."

The vicar had also remained in the same line of work, though his position as curate had an air of punishment for stealing from the tithe.

"The blackmailer knew of my sinful proclivity. I had been jailed for it before I joined the clergy," Reverend Livingstone said as he dusted the altar. "But forgiveness is the core of the church."

"But you didn't want the village to know?" I asked.

"I wanted to remain. I loved that area. Did you know there were all kinds of underground caves and tunnels in the region? I would often hike around trying to find entrances..."

"Mr. Patton thought he spotted you on that day...," said Holmes.

"I think I saw him too, heading to the village just after dusk. Didn't see the policeman, though."

On the train back to Ferndene, I expressed bafflement. "Did the policeman lie and take the money himself? Perhaps split it with Patton?"

Holmes smiled. "The answer is less prosaic. Though it does involve collaboration."

Question: Who does Holmes suspect stole the blackmail money?

Hint: Spare uniform.

5 The Wrong Victim

"**S**even years ago, when I was working as a waitress at the tea house, I was poor and desperate, but that doesn't excuse my actions," said Phyllis Plum, sadly. "When Mr. Blue asked me to put that powder in his friend's drink, 'as a joke,' I knew it must have been poison, but I needed the money, so I agreed. Mr. Blue's cup was blue, and Dr. Stanners' red, and I poured the powder into the red cup. It dissolved instantly with no smell. I gave them the cups and watched like a hawk! They both drained their cups as they talked and then... Mr. Blue keeled over!"

Her face was a mix of horror and confusion.

"People rushed over, but his heart had stopped instantly. Mr. Stanners looked shocked, but healthy! How?"

"Are certain you put the powder in the red cup, and Mr. Stanners drank from it?" asked Holmes.

"Certain. The police tested the cups afterward and found no poison in either one!"

"They didn't believe your confession?"

"They thought I just wanted attention. Dr. Stanners was insistent Mr. Blue had a heart problem and that I was confused."

Holmes tested the cups with his own techniques. They were provided by Inspector Bradstreet.

"She's a fantasist. Pinched her for theft two years earlier. She claimed a cat had 'knocked' a

necklace into her purse," said Bradstreet. "Blue had a heart attack; she made up this poison story for attention."

"But then, why say Mr. Blue had her put something in Dr. Stanners' cup?" I interjected. "Why not say Dr. Stanners had her poison Mr. Blue?"

Bradstreet mulled this over. "Well, Dr. Stanners was respected in the community, whereas Blue was a... poet. He was a laudanum user. Heart problems. No surprise how he died," Bradstreet said.

"Who said he had heart problems? Doctor Stanners?" queried Holmes.

"Well, yes..." said Bradstreet, looking uncomfortable.

Holmes stood up. "I've completed my examination, and I must concur there is no evidence of poison in either cup."

Bradstreet looked smug.

"I detected trace elements of some compound in the red cup. I cannot identify it at this moment but that lends credence to Miss Plum's story."

Dr. Stephen Stanners kept offices on Harley Street, and readily agreed to talk to us.

"Benjamin's death was very upsetting, and the young woman's story only made it worse," he said sombrely. "I'm happy to provide any files you would like to prove his health problems. People were always making up scandalous stories about him, and if I'm honest he sometimes liked them. But I refuse to have his name denigrated after his death."

"An odd friendship, wasn't it? An indigent poet and a well-respected doctor?" asked Holmes.

"As odd as that between you and Dr. Watson?" said Dr. Stanners. "I'm joking, of course. Benjamin and I knew each other from birth. He was my best friend; we shared all our highs and lows."

That last phrase brought an expression of deep melancholy across the doctor's face.

"Had you spent time together that day before going to the tea house?" asked Holmes.

"Yes, we had met here at my office earlier, to discuss recent events."

"His wife had left him that morning, I believe? And yours had recently passed?"

Stanners looked annoyed at Holmes' knowledge of his private life.

"Yes. But we were not... we were in good spirits. And we decided it was better to continue our conversation at the tea house."

Holmes leaned forward.

"Dr. Stanners, I should inform you that my tests showed that there were traces of some as yet unidentified substance in your teacup, the red one."

Stanners frowned. "Really? I cannot think what it would be. Perhaps something left by the previous test?"

"I would hope you would credit me the wherewithal of having compensated for that, Dr. Stanners," Holmes said with an annoyed tone. "Whatever it was, it was present that day."

"Well, I hate to say it, but perhaps the young lady was responsible for that," replied Stanners, but his voice was unconvincing.

"Have you any experience with poisons, Dr. Stanners?" asked Holmes innocently, even though all assembled knew the answer.

"I have written several papers on the subject that you yourself have mentioned in print, Mr. Holmes," said Dr. Stanners, his manner getting icier by the second. "I will however note that my expertise is in curing poisons, not administering them. Now, if you don't mind, I have a patient waiting."

As we left the office, Holmes smiled with surprising warmth.

"It's remarkable, Watson, the way this case reflects both the foolishness and the nobility of the common man."

"Do you know who the murderer is?"

"In a way. But I also know someone for whom the reverse is true..."

Question: Who does Holmes think killed Mr. Blue, and how?

Hint: Cure.

6 The Scowling Face

"**M**y grandfather Arthur moved to Wyoming from England and made a fortune selling snake oil," said Alexander Kingsley, outside a supposedly haunted shack. "Bunkum of the worst kind. My father, Bromwell Kingsley, refused the tainted money. He returned to England only to find grandfather had fooled him too. His father has said the family was gentry, but it turned out they were mere peasant farmers on a Lord's land..."

"The tale of how your father moved into this hovel, built his empire and bought this estate is well known," said Holmes.

Bromwell Kingsley died 12 years ago, and his will stipulated that his son, Alexander, could only inherit his fortune if he spent one night in the shack, otherwise it would be split between his mother and their lawyer. Bromwell claimed his father, Arthur, had gambled away his money, returned to England and died.

"His ghost supposedly joined the others in the shack. My father intended for me to stay there as a test. I was sure I was brave... until that night."

A week later, Alexander prepared to go to the shack, bidding his mother goodnight. She lives in Hattonfield, the Lord's mansion bought by Bromwell once he had enough money.

"Mother wasn't worried. She never believed father's stories; she'd never had time for his superstitions. Mr. Fancher, the lawyer, was there to ensure I remained inside the entire night. I waved and headed into the shack."

He paused.

"It was small and cold, but while wandering I've slept in mud huts, and fields. Then I saw the face. It hung in the air, scowling. It moved toward me, spinning; blood and insects pouring from its eyes! No wires or glass plates either. I bolted through the front door."

The Kingsley inheritance passed to his mother and Fancher. The police had suppressed the case to protect Alexander Kingsley's reputation.

"Shall we go inside?" I asked Holmes.

"Unnecessary," he said, without elaborating.

Calliope Kingsley seemed made of gossamer, her pale thin figure surrounded by wispy curtains.

"My son's travels and adventures may have bolstered his bravado, but he was not prepared for that shack," she said croakily.

"You believe it was a ghost?" asked Holmes.

"Yes. I see no other explanation. If anyone had a spirit evil enough to become a phantom, it was Arthur Kingsley..."

"Did you ever meet your husband's father?" asked Holmes.

"Not personally, but he loomed large in Bromwell's memory. Bromwell said when he was angry his smile disappeared and his face became a scowling mask, just as my son described."

"Did you see his face as he left the shack?" said Holmes.

"I fear both I and Mr. Fancher had fallen asleep by then. Ironically Alexander could have lied and got the money. But he woke us minutes after he had left. My son is very honest. I was determined to ensure he had his father's money to protect him, but no mother can protect their child from the supernatural."

Mr. Fancher waited in the next room and seemed like a man in middle age who was impatient to be old, with a bald head and a stooped back.

"When Bromwell Kingsley told me of this ridiculous scheme for his will, I tried everything to persuade him otherwise!" he said with vitality. "He was always so sensible in his business dealings; this kind of... prank eluded me."

"You don't think he believed in the ghost?" I asked.

"Oh, he'd tell the story often enough, but I thought it mere jocularity. Perhaps he intended it to be the full stop on the life of his notorious father, with his very spirit confronted and rejected by his grandson. But it did not turn out that way."

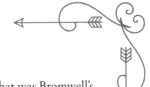

"It benefited you somewhat, though," replied Holmes pointedly.

Fancher bristled at this. "I never asked to be given any money! But that was Bromwell's wish, and I must follow my clients' instructions, even if they are not to my liking."

Fancher's waistcoat and pocket-watch suggested to me that he was not entirely unhappy with how events unfolded...

"Did you see him leave the shack? Mrs. Kingsley said you were asleep..."

He was annoyed by this suggestion.

"She was, and I may have dozed, but as he left he gave such a wail! I saw him bolt out, eyes squinting and his teeth gritted, like he was trying to fight the fear deep within him, or maybe he was tensing his body against the freezing cold creeping through his blood!"

Holmes nodded thoughtfully, and then excused us.

"I suppose we should search the shack, think about how it was done. A projection, like those magic lantern shows? Or perhaps a hallucination, induced with some kind of drug?" I suggested.

"Consider this: 'Like father, like son,'" said Holmes.

Question: Who does Holmes suspect was responsible for the Scowling Face?

7   The Magic Key

"One year ago, a masked man walked into Arnold Finch Goldsmiths in broad daylight and emptied the safe. I didn't have a clue," said Inspector Freep.

"Until Mrs. St-John visited the station?" asked Holmes.

"Yes. She was a customer inside when it happened. But she spins a tale about this magic key."

Mrs. St-John claimed the robber had reached into her bag and produced... the key to the safe!

"But Mrs. St-John is not a... reliable witness," continued the Inspector. "Neither the clerk nor the owner's wife saw it happen. Mrs. St-John said he returned it, and when she got home it had vanished! I stamped the file with an A and tried to forget it."

"Either the clerk or the owner's wife, Mrs. Finch, could have slipped the key into her bag," Holmes said. "Or Mrs. St-John is the accomplice. There's no prior connection between her and the shop."

When we met with her, Mrs. St-John seemed rather absentminded.

"Sorry about the teapot, I've been in the garden," she said, holding a pot plant.

It seemed she initially didn't recognize the maid but then ordered her to get us some tea.

"I had never seen the key before in my life!" she said. "I was so stunned that when the police chap was asking this and that, I didn't mention it. It all seemed like a dream. Especially as I couldn't find it once I returned here."

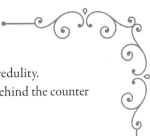

"You didn't mention it to Mrs. Finch or the clerk?" I asked with incredulity.

"They seemed frightened by the robber chap's knife. The clerk was behind the counter and the woman was waving her hands around."

"Do you still have the bag?" asked Holmes.

"I have it in here!" she said, opening a cupboard and producing a vase.

"No, wait... I traded the purse with Bunty Greenleaf for this vase because I kept being followed by bees when I was in the park," she said merrily. "It's a shame; it was the only one I had that would take all my toiletries and hand-fan. Plus, it matched my red hat."

Holmes decided further questioning would be fruitless, so we went to Arnold Finch's shop to speak to the clerk and Mrs. Finch.

"After the robbery, we struggled to recover," Mrs. Finch said bitterly. She seemed a hard-edged, sober woman, the opposite of Mrs. St-John.

"We were lucky that we were able to secure supportive funding from a childhood friend of mine, Nigel Bickerstaff. He has been kind enough to become a silent partner in the business; he didn't even ask for his name to be put on the sign!"

"So you didn't recognize the robber, or see him get the key from Mrs. St-John?" asked Holmes.

"No... although now you mention it, I did see him touch her bag once, but I thought nothing of it at the time. I was quite frightened; I held as still as possible."

"But you didn't think he was working with her?"

Mrs. Finch shook her head.

"Mrs. St-John is a sweet girl with far too much money, not a criminal."

She then leaned forward.

"I have had my suspicions about our clerk, Mark. He loves to bet on the dogs. If anyone would need money..."

A short man entered the shop, immediately speaking to Mrs. Finch.

"Dearest, the butcher's boy needs paying."

"It's in my bag, Arnold," she said evenly, pointing into the office. The man disappeared inside.

"This one?" he said out of sight.

"No, the bigger one, with the poppies."

We then spoke with the young clerk, Mark Norris.

"At first, I didn't even realize what was happening! Mrs. St-John had accidentally knocked into the brass scales and had put her bag down to try to help pick up the pieces, but she was getting very confused so Mrs. Finch, who had come in to get her reticule, had to try and help her, so when there was suddenly this man with a mask and knife in front of us, I barely knew what to do!"

"Did you see him get the key from Mrs. St-John?" asked Holmes.

"No, I had crouched down somewhat. I wasn't the only one who was afraid. Mrs. Finch was waving her hands around, swapping right to left and vice versa. When the robber saw that, I thought he would attack her to keep her quiet."

Holmes nodded. "After he had emptied the safe and gone, what happened?"

"Well, we were all shocked. The ladies picked up their bags and we went outside to summon a policeman."

As we left the store, I asked Holmes why he didn't ask Mr. Norris about his gambling.

"That was an irrelevant detail, Watson."

"So, you don't suspect him?"

"I didn't say that, Watson. But I do now understand the appearance and disappearance of the 'magic' key, and the identity of the robber's accomplice..."

Question: Who does Holmes suspect of being the robber's accomplice?

Hint: Bag

8 The Final Escape

Selsey Pleasure Pier had always struggled to draw visitors. But in the playhouse at its end, The Great Chanticleer had stepped into a box on stage and disappeared... forever!

As this information had been sent to the Archive, it had almost been forgotten.

"Eight years hence," said Henry O'Malley, Chanticleer's assistant, a rosy-cheeked Irishman with a thick accent. "T'weren't a grand crowd that day, to be sure. But still, he gave the same amazing performance. After the old doves act, there was the finale: I'd haul the box on stage, leave it. Chanticleer comes on next and gets inside, and shuts it. Ten seconds later it opens, and by the saints he's gone! Five seconds later he appears behind them! But this time... nothin'."

O'Malley had agreed to meet us in a cafe near the pier, having spent eight years touring Britain with his own act. He seemed to be acting even as we spoke, his "jolly Irishman" disposition broad and exaggerated.

"We searched the whole place, then the town. Nothin'. His final, greatest trick."

"How did it usually work?" I asked.

"Are ye in the magic circle? I can't give away the secret, boyo," he said, winking at Holmes.

"Chanticleer had quite a few debtors?" asked Holmes. "They were very interested in finding him."

O'Malley bristled.

"Charles was a respectable fella. He'd never skip out on anyone, begorrah! I think he sick, not long for this world, so he created an illusion to stand for all time!"

"Some say that you would quarrel a lot," said Holmes.

"Oh, to be sure, we had a few barnies, but he taught me everything! It was they who didn't care for him, that greasy playhouse manager Kinton, and that thuggish stagehand Fred Bax."

We decided to head to the playhouse, but O'Malley declined to come, saying there were too many memories.

"Chanticleer was a has-been," said Fred Bax, now stage manager. "Borrowed money from everyone, even I lent him some! He owed most to Mr. Kinton. That's why he disappeared. More than crabs in the water under this pier."

Sherlock examined the playhouse's aisle and then leaped onto the stage.

"Do you understand the trick, Mr. Bax?" Holmes asked.

Bax nodded. "Chanticleer kept schtum, 'magic circle,' but O'Malley told me after a drink. Trapdoor in the stage, box on top of it. Chanticleer goes in, drops through, runs along the corridor under the seats, pops out through that door announcing himself," he said, pointing to the back of the auditorium.

Standing on the stage, Holmes kicked it sharply and vanished! Bax rushed forward.

"Careful! If you're too heavy, you smack your head on the edge!"

Two minutes later, Holmes emerged from the side door, out of breath. Bax and I ran over.

"It's quite a dash," Holmes panted. "Was Mr. Chanticleer athletic?"

"He was very thin," Bax said. "But not very muscular with it. Too much time in boxes, I suppose. O'Malley was the same, must have been a magician thing."

"Has anything been repaired below the stage since the disappearance?" Holmes said.

"Dunno. I only became manager two years ago; I wasn't allowed under the stage before then."

The office of the owner, Mr. Kinton, was as windy as the sea front, and he sat behind his desk with an appropriately fish-like expression and scent.

"I hate magicians," he said, leaning over his desk. "I always wanted to have a music hall. But I was told magic was the real money-spinner. Pfft. The only thing Chanticleer disappeared was my profits."

"You lent him money?" said Holmes.

"Said he had an idea for an amazing trick that would make the headlines! Tsk."

"Did you see the act?" I asked.

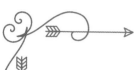

"Yes, I stupidly thought he had something new. But it was the same old nonsense with him in his turban and cloak, climbing inside the box. When I realized he'd gone, I was furious.

"Then the police say we can't even talk about it. That day I fired O'Malley and had all the magic paraphernalia cleared out!"

"O'Malley took the box?" I asked.

"Said he would try to carry on the act in Chanticleer's name. What a joke. They hated each other," said Kinton. "That's what I heard, anyway. Always kept myself away from the performers. But I heard them once going at it, Chanticleer shouting at O'Malley about eating too much. Or was it the other way round? No, it was Chanticleer; O'Malley was Irish."

"Hmm," said Holmes, his usual doubtful noise.

After we left, Holmes waded as far underneath the pier as he could and produced a small set of field glasses, using them to look at the underside of the pier. He handed them to me and directed me to look at a patch of wood right at the end, a different shade to the rest.

"What does it mean?" I asked.

"It means 'Eureka!,' Watson. Or should I say, 'Abracadabra?'"

Question: Who does Sherlock Holmes suspect is responsible for the disappearance?

Hint: Switch.

9 The Unbreakable Code

Roderick Lassiter was an importer... officially. But he was obviously actually a spy.

"Mr. Holmes!" Lassiter roared as we entered. "Sorry to hear about..."

"Tell us about this robbery," interrupted Holmes. I wondered what Lassiter was going to say.

"Three years ago, while abroad, I sustained a bullet to the shoulder while... walking," he said. "I decided to return to London, run my business and spend time with my son Jacob. Two weeks later, someone ransacks my office! Smashed window. Took three fountain pens and the petty cash. Nothing important like our records or account books. Then we found this..."

He showed us a piece of paper that had written on it a string of numbers in a loose but neat hand:

1 2 3 4 5 6 7 8 9 1 2 6 9 111111 222222 666666 999999 29292929

"We have foreign competitors. It seemed logical it could be a message written in code, dropped from the burglar's pocket."

Holmes peered at the numbers.

"We all had a go at deciphering it. Myself, Jacob, my secretary Mr. Greg Morrison, and our young clerk Lancelot Creegan. But it proved impossible to crack! We even bounced it... upstairs. Their best boffins were stumped. So the whole thing got swept under the carpet."

"I need handwriting samples from your son, Mr. Morrison, and Mr. Creegan," Holmes said sharply.

"You suspect them?" said Lassiter. "They would never collude with the enemy."

"You understand the benefit of gathering data."

"Fine, but you can ask them yourself. Graphology? Nonsense."

Lassiter's secretary, Gregory Morrison, aped Lassiter with his rakish grin and manner.

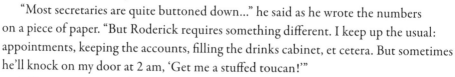

"Most secretaries are quite buttoned down..." he said as he wrote the numbers on a piece of paper. "But Roderick requires something different. I keep up the usual: appointments, keeping the accounts, filling the drinks cabinet, et cetera. But sometimes he'll knock on my door at 2 am, 'Get me a stuffed toucan!'"

"Were you concerned when your office was robbed?" said Holmes.

"If I am honest it took me a moment to realize. I wasn't keeping it spick and span. I'm behind on a few tasks."

"What about the code?" asked Holmes.

"No luck. It's damned near impossible to solve those things with no key. Don't have a head for ciphers myself, but I've had to adapt."

"And Jacob Lassiter and Mr. Creegan helped?"

"Creegan was keen but lacked experience. Jacob's done a course on code-breaking, but he lost interest quite quickly."

Unlike Mr. Morrison, Jacob Lassiter seemed the opposite of his father. His clothing was neat and reserved, his voice was quiet and measured.

"A writing sample? Of course. I have studied graphology extensively," he said. "I can imagine what my father said about this, though."

Jacob launched into a remarkable impersonation of his father.

"Handwriting?" he blustered. "Balderdash!"

"You have a knack for imitation!" I said admiringly.

"I studied acting four years ago. I have no natural skills but if I study for long enough, I can turn my hand to anything. But I cannot settle. Journalism, accountancy, cartography..."

"Your father funds your quest for purpose?" Holmes asked.

"He did, then he decided I needed more life experience. Hence my work at his company."

"Do you like Mr. Morrison and Mr. Creegan?"

"Lancelot Creegan's an OK sort, rather dry, but Mr. Morrison would do better to spend less time trying to be father. The whole code business was a handy distraction from the tasks he hasn't done."

Lancelot Creegan briefly reminded me of a younger Moriarty, with his chalk-stained jacket and beetle brow, but without the perspicacity. He seemed totally unaware of Roderick Lassiter's true occupation.

"I am often frustrated with the business's operation, Mr. Holmes. Mr. Lassiter has many connections, but he'll often return from abroad without even a purchase order. Jacob Lassiter is never here, and Mr. Morrison runs a very loose ship."

Holmes asked Creegan to write the numbers down.

"Ah yes, the cipher!" he uttered. "A fascinating thing, not Alberti or pigpen, or many other possibilities. Quite uncrackable."

"Didn't you think it strange that a coded message would be used by someone burgling a simple office?" I asked.

"No, I just assumed the culprit was an enthusiast, like me."

Once Holmes had the samples, we returned to Baker Street, and he began his comparison with the original paper. Several hours later he stood up, smiling.

"Just as I thought."

"Have you cracked the code, Holmes?" I asked.

"If you mean, do I understand what is written on this paper, yes," said Holmes cryptically. "But it was the handwriting analysis that achieved that outcome."

"So, it was written by one of our suspects?" I said.

"Watson, the handwriting on this page does not match one of our suspects. But one of them wrote it."

Question: Who does Holmes suspect is responsible for burgling the office?

Hint: Practice.

10   The Forgotten Folly

Three years ago, Freddy Faber seemingly gave his entire fortune to a stranger, then claimed he had never done it. The news spread quickly but then died out soon after.

"I thought it odd but as I was 'dead' I could not investigate. Now through this file I have learned that Mr. Faber said he was captive for three months while an imposter took his place," said Holmes, peering at a beaker of dirt.

Faber claimed he had been strolling through Mayfair when he was knocked out. He awoke, hooded, in a carriage. He was thrown out, marched across mud, and then pushed into a small space.

"I ripped the hood off and saw some kind of hexagonal stone room," Faber had told the police. "It was quite cold, but I had a blanket. There was one small triangular window, but I could only see trees. Someone unseen slid a tray of food and water once a day, under the door. I only saw three people that entire time, but none of them seemed to hear me. Then one morning I just awoke back home. My lawyer told it was three months later and I'd given everything away!"

The police convinced Faber to keep his ridiculous story silent to protect what remained of his dignity.

"But I think the unimaginative Mr. Faber may be telling the truth. I can think of several criminals who could impersonate him."

He held up a shoe.

"My tests show the dirt on his footwear originates from the New Forest, specifically the part within Hampshire. I'm certain I know where he was kept."

Half a day later we stood in the forest in front of a small turret with no castle attached.

"Lord Daleforth's folly," said Holmes declaratively. "When he owned this land, he had it built as a gift for his wife. She hated it, so it stands forgotten."

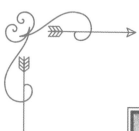

Everything about it matched Faber's description. It had to be the spot.

We returned to the nearby village of Minstead where the constable had rounded up three locals who matched Faber's descriptions.

"It must be a local; a stranger would stand out too much," said Holmes.

First was a Gilbert Dial, a handsome young gentleman with green eyes that suggested he was thinking of a cruel joke.

"I was in the area," he said dismissively. "My horse, Baldur, has a penchant for the apples that grow on the trees. I must have been picking some when Mr. Faber saw me. He's lucky he only saw the inside of that eyesore."

"You didn't hear his shouts for help?" asked Holmes.

"Perhaps I may have. But there are screeching foxes in that area, not to mention owls."

"Did you see anyone else?" asked Holmes.

"Sometimes I see that old Mr. Smit wandering around," said Dial. "Avoiding his wife's nagging probably. I live up in Dial Hall, I don't interact with... locals."

Second was Ethel Ramsdon, a harried looking young woman.

"I feel a perfect fool," she said tearfully. "I could have helped that young man but only cared for my feelings!"

"You heard him?" Holmes asked.

"Perhaps. I had gone into the forest because my ex-fiancée gave me a St. Valentine's present with another girl's name on it," she said angrily.

"He gave someone else a gift?" I asked.

"I was so incensed I was determined to go and bury the rotten thing in the forest. But the ground was too frozen for the shovel. While there I did hear a kind of faint 'help me.' But I thought it was my imagination."

"Did you see anyone else there?" Holmes asked.

"I don't think so," she said, frowning.

After confirming with the constable that Ethel had "broken it off" with a young man, we spoke to Pieter Smit, our final suspect. He stroked his bushy white beard as we explained.

"What is it you do in this area, Mr. Smit?" Holmes asked.

"Oh, this and that," he said in a soft Dutch accent. "Repairs, mending. Sometimes I like to walk in the woods."

"Near the folly?" said Holmes.

"Ah, yes. Well, on this occasion I think I was not looking at nature. I had argued with my wife over dinner. The feast of Sinterklaas was coming, but my wife did not want to celebrate; said the locals only cared for 'Father Christmas.' So I was angry, and I wanted to shout and not be heard. It is a shame; I think your young man was also shouting and I did not hear him over my own voice..."

"Yes, Mr. Faber did say you were shouting. Did you see anyone else?" asked Holmes.

"I saw perhaps that young man Mr. Dial. He was walking from that place carrying something, but I did not see what, as it was getting dark," Mr. Smit said, shrugging.

Mr. Smit was dismissed, and Holmes lit a pipe.

"The guilty party is obvious. Ironic that their whole scheme could unravel over such a simple lie," said Holmes, shaking his head.

Question: Who does Holmes suspect was working with Faber's captors?

Hint: Season.

11 The Blackmailed Blackguard

"Jeremiah Crookshank was a money-grubbing skinflint," said Graham Forster. "But I owe it to him to catch his blackmailer."

Crookshank had amassed a vast fortune through vicious amorality and exploiting others' fear of him. He died with no friends and an estranged family. After his death, a large chunk of his fortune seemed to be missing.

"It was my job to monitor all of Mr. Crookshank's investments," said Forster.

"It still is," said Holmes. "His dark reputation has kept his business going rather healthily in his absence, I understand."

"Mr. Crookshank had been secretly visiting a post office box in a village in Essex, leaving large sums of money there."

"You suspect blackmail?" asked Holmes.

"Naturally I informed the police, but then I heard nothing for years!"

The force had turned up three people who had visited the box, and had then decided to Archive the case as they all had spotless reputations, and any scandal could have ruined their lives.

First was Mary Haldon, author of instructional books for women that Holmes had remarked were surprisingly useful. She was a plain-spoken woman who seemed rather amused by it all.

"Yes, I visited that post office. I was posting a letter," she said.

"To whom?" asked Holmes.

"That's private," she said bluntly. "I depend on real-life tips from women. If I exposed their identities, they would stop sending tips, and I'd have to write the same pabulum as others."

"Do you pay these women?" said Holmes.

"I share my profits," Miss Haldon said.

"Did you ever meet Mr. Crookshank?" Holmes asked.

"He visited my office to tell me women shouldn't write or read. Complained to my publishers," she said.

"So, you had a good reason to hate him? And a broad source of information?" said Holmes.

"Everyone hated him," Miss Haldon responded. "Yet few knew anything about him. That was his power."

The second person was Dr. Peter Golden. We found him in a tiny clinic in Limehouse in the process of giving smallpox vaccinations. There was a reluctance amongst the locals, but Golden's warm smile and charm was winning some of them over.

"Crookshank, oh my goodness!" Golden said when we spoke to him. "What a horror. He found out I was trying to vaccinate his workers in Manchester, personally came to the clinic and told me I was working for one of his rivals, trying to poison his men."

"And he stopped you?"

Golden paused. "He tried, but by that point I had already administered most of the injections."

"How do you fund your activities, Mr. Golden?" Holmes asked. "Your daily itinerary seems to leave little time for paying patients."

"You would be surprised how easily funds can be acquired," Golden said, and for the first time his smile had an aspect of falsity.

"And your reason for being in Coggeshall post office?" I asked.

"I was there to vaccinate the staff," he said, refusing to be drawn further. It seemed odd he would travel all that way for such a small task.

The final suspect was Josephine DeBauvau, a young French woman who worked as a teacher in Finsbury. Her school seemed rather well appointed for the area, and we were equally surprised when we realized all her students had ailments of various sorts.

"The little ones, they struggle so much outside these walls, so I try to make this place a sanctuary for them, and also to improve their minds," she said in a soft French accent,

a tear welling in her eye. She made the suffering heroine in a melodrama look like one of Macbeth's witches.

"And how did you find yourself in a post office frequented by Jeremiah Crookshank?" asked Holmes, whose natural cynicism seemed to be wilting in the heat of Miss DeBauvau's saintlike aura.

"Oh, that... terrible man!" she said, although she seemed to have difficulty saying it. "He owned the lease on this school and said he would triple the rent. Throw us all out on the street. What a mean old gentleman."

"And the post office?" said Holmes, trying to bring us back to the subject.

"Oh yes. I was posting a letter," she said warily.

"That seems to be a popular activity there," said Holmes ironically.

"If you gentlemen do not mind, I have a lesson in two minutes, so..."

As we left the school, Holmes was chuckling to himself in a very good-natured way.

"I don't see what's so amusing," I said. "They all seem too good to be true. But one of them must not be. Or even all of them. It sickens me to think of the damage we might do to their reputation if we get it wrong."

"Indeed, Watson, reputation is the key word here," said Holmes. "Your statements are a mix of right and wrong. But don't worry. I know exactly what has happened."

Question: Who does Holmes suspect of blackmailing Jeremiah Crookshank?

Hint: Reputation.

12 The College Poisoner

"We must hurry, Watson!" said Holmes as we rushed onto the Cambridge train. I soon understood once Holmes explained. Two years ago, there had been a series of strange illnesses at St. Julian's in Cambridge, one of the few all-girl's colleges. No one had died, but several girls left, suffering continued health problems. The college asked the police to suppress the case as they knew the press would have a field day with it.

"Foolish," said Holmes. "As I have heard a new rash of similar cases has struck there. It's poison, I'm sure."

We arrived and spoke to the college's Mistress, Charlotte Hall. She informed Holmes that three women currently at the college had also been there during the first incidents.

"I care deeply about the safety of my girls," she said defensively. "But I was discouraged from taking it further."

We were permitted to speak to the women while they were having lunch in the cramped Main Hall. They were all residents.

The first woman was Mary Catford, who was warily poking her boiled beef with a fork. She seemed unconcerned with appearing ladylike, leaning her elbows on the table as if challenging us to comment.

"I'm studying the Maths Tripos. Well, not officially. None of us are," she said bitterly. "We're not allowed to sit the real exam. But to all intents and purposes."

"Do you know anyone who has suffered from this illness?" asked Holmes.

"Of course! There's few enough of us here anyway. Alice, Mary, the other Mary…"

"Is there any evident animosity between students here?" Holmes asked.

"No! Well…" said Mary, and then leaned forward.

"There's always a bit of sniping back and forth. It's natural. I'm always saying we should keep our powder dry for when we must go up against men, but we're only human. If you're

asking do I think one of us would murder anyone, no."

"You worked at a restaurant where there was a similar incident," said Holmes. "The Maison Jaune in Brighton."

"The chef there sent out roast chicken so undercooked it was clucking," she replied defensively. "I don't work in the kitchens here."

"You have access," said Holmes.

"We all do. We don't have many staff so we wash and put away our own cutlery and plates," she said, and with that in mind she pushed her uneaten beef to the side.

The second woman was Katherine Dagworthy. She seemed much more frightened than Miss Catford, but also more dedicated to decorum, sitting up straight in her seat and refusing to speak whenever she ate a mouthful of food.

"I'm not surprised that there's a murderer," she whispered. "You should see some of the looks the girls give each other over the slightest things."

"Who in particular?" Holmes asked.

"I don't like to gossip," Miss Dagworthy said, before taking a dainty sip of water. "I'm probably guilty of a grumpy look or two. I'm not sure an all-women's college is a good idea. All this emotion bottled up in one place."

"What do you study?" asked Holmes.

"English. The truth is I heard that wealthy eligible bachelors prefer women who are a little versed in the arts. I'm sure you understand."

"So, you have no idea who it might be?" I asked.

"Well, Millicent did tell Mary, not Mary H, Mary C, that she'd heard she poisoned some people in Brighton. And Mary C was livid. But that was after the illnesses started, so I don't suppose that counts."

Millicent Smythe disputed Miss Dagworthy's characterization of the encounter.

"I merely remarked to Mary Catford that perhaps she might have an idea of what was making people sick, as she had previous experience in this regard," she said coolly. "You can ask Mary if you want; Katherine has a tendency to embroider these things somewhat."

"So, you think these are just cases of gastrointestinal disorder?" queried Holmes.

"I haven't the foggiest. I am simply trying... no, thank you!" she said as someone tried to put a plate of food down in front of her. "I am simply trying to finish my time of studying here so I can get a decent job. Sometimes I feel a lot of the women here would be happy to study forever."

As we left the hall, I imagined Holmes would now want to search all their rooms, dust the kitchen for prints and do a scientific analysis of every suspicious speck in the place. But instead, he merely crossed his arms and said, "I'm almost disappointed how easy this has been, Watson. But at least we can now prevent a tragedy."

"You already know who's doing it?" I said, confused.

"Of course. In this case actions spoke louder than words."

Question: Who does Sherlock Holmes suspect of the poisonings?

Hint: Eating.

13 The Six Notes

The three identical notes bore an illustrated Grim Reaper next to a spidery scrawl:

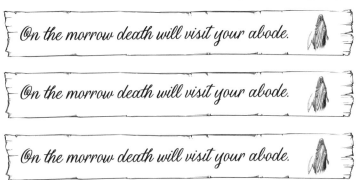

On the morrow death will visit your abode.

On the morrow death will visit your abode.

On the morrow death will visit your abode.

"Three people received this note. They left their house and it was burgled," said Inspector Stanley Hopkins. "Inspector Cake sent it to the Archive because he was retiring and didn't want to deal with it."

Holmes suspected one of the victims was the perpetrator.

Muriel Fike's seemed remarkably limber for her age.

"I eat only vegetables, exercise regularly," she said. "I don't fear Death, I refuse to let it win." She held the note.

"I regret leaving the house that day. But I couldn't ignore the omen."

Mrs. Fike's house was filled with paintings and drawings of skulls.

"Who do you think sent it?" asked Holmes.

"Local children? They mock my skulls," she said. "I rarely see Brom Brown, who lives next door; sometimes I hear him and his friends carousing. Liam McFee, I see occasionally, in his ridiculous garb."

"He's an undertaker," Hopkins commented to Holmes. Holmes scrawled something on a piece of paper and showed it to Hopkins, who nodded.

"How can you afford this house, Mrs. Fike? Unmarried, no inheritance..." said Holmes.

"I was bequeathed it by one of my converts to vegetarianism," she said proudly.

Brom Brown was a career criminal. He had crossed our paths a few times. But he had a plausible excuse for not being the author of the notes.

"Can't read or write," he said bluntly. "Never needed to."

"If you couldn't read the note, why did you do as it told?" I asked.

"The picture of the Reaper scared the life out of me. I had a friend read it and I was off. I looked a prize plum when I was robbed."

"You do not strike me as an easily scared man," said Holmes dryly.

"I've always been scared of the Reaper," Brown said. "My dad used to lock me in a cupboard which had this old story book. I stared at that bony face many a time."

"Indeed," said Holmes. He scrawled something on a piece of paper and put it on the table in front of Hopkins, who read it.

"Did you suspect anyone nearby?" asked Holmes.

"That old lady has a house filled with skulls and skeletons!" he said, wide-eyed. "And the other bloke, he's an undertaker. Just my luck to live here."

"Yes, most unfortunate," said Holmes, knocking on the table. Brown flinched considerably.

"Do you think...?" began Holmes, but he was interrupted by Hopkins suddenly giving the most blood-curdling cry I have ever heard. Mr. Brown seemed shocked.

"What, what is it?"

"Sorry," said Hopkins, visibly shaken. "Thought I saw something. This whole case has unsettled me."

Hopkins' bizarre turn seemed to leave him unaffected, as when we went to visit the undertaker he looked as stolid as ever.

The young man we met, Liam McFee, looked more like a poet, not at all like a typical undertaker.

"I didn't leave the house because of the note!" he said, offended. "I deal with the dead

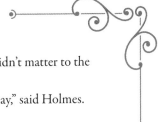

all the time. I left because I was called to collect a body. Of course, it didn't matter to the burglar why I left; they struck all the same."

"I spoke to your father, and he said you had no engagements that day," said Holmes.

McFee stuttered.

"He... father must be mistaken. He is losing his faculties. That's why he is making me... why I am preparing to take over the business."

"I see," said Holmes. He now showed a piece of paper to McFee alone.

"What do you make of this?" he asked.

McFee's face went totally white, and he almost leaped out of his chair.

"Oh no! Where did you find that?" he croaked.

"I wrote it myself. It's a passable imitation of the original, don't you think?" said Holmes airily.

McFee's face went from white to red and he looked quite angry. Holmes, however, looked quite satisfied and we all left.

"The culprit wrote three notes, Watson, and now with three notes of my own I have caught them," said Holmes. "Take a look."

He showed me the three pieces of paper: One had "MY BONY FINGERS SHALL CHOKE YOU TONIGHT" written on it in the same hand as the death notes. The second was a drawing of a skull that looked a little, but not much, like the Grim Reaper. And the third was written in Holmes' own hand (though larger than usual) and said, "When I knock on the table please give the most terrifying scream you can muster."

I do not know what order he used the notes in, but Holmes was confident he had solved the case.

Question: Who does Sherlock Holmes think sent the notes and robbed the houses?

14 The Cask of Ale

Creaser's Ales has supplied beverages to public houses across the North of England for decades. When their York factory was built 20 years ago, the opening was marred by the disappearance of Horace Creaser, company founder and figurehead.

"His son and inheritor Peter was the main suspect. But the business has struggled without 'Grandpa Creaser,' so I doubt it was him," said Holmes as we entered the empty factory. "Then, I read that two years ago they had to reinforce a waterlogged wall in the eastern wing."

We headed straight there. Iron bars had been used to shore up the wall. I saw why. The bricks were uneven, and the mortar more sloppily applied than the surrounding walls.

Holmes broke the wall with first swing of his sledgehammer, revealing the desiccated corpse of Horace Creaser!

Holmes insisted this be kept on a need-to-know basis. He performed various tests, concluding that Creaser had been walled up shortly before the brewery's completion. This meant that only three people could have been responsible: Thomas Gunter, head of the construction company, who completed the final inspection unaccompanied; Cecil Moncrieff, the architect, who always took a lone walk through the buildings he had designed after completion; and Phyllis Tandforth, the landscape gardener, who had been single-handedly building a small, enclosed garden for Horace Creaser.

Gunter, now wealthy, said he hadn't lifted a trowel in years. We visited him at his mansion.

"I can't say I didn't take pride in the work I did and oversaw," he said. "But it was just a job. Managing is just as hard."

Holmes had only told him that we were investigating Creaser's disappearance.

"I was surprised that old swine wouldn't come and cut the ribbon. The building was

his new toy and he'd been there every day complaining. I think he missed bullying his workers,"

"He had no other breweries?" I asked.

"No. Then he said he wouldn't pay us as we'd done such a bad job. His son was a better sort; gave us the money immediately."

"What do you think happened to Horace?" Holmes asked.

"I reckon he tried some new batch of ale and fell into the Ouse!" laughed Gunter.

"Did you see anything odd during your final inspection?"

"No. Creaser told me Moncrieff wanted his little visit, told me to hurry up. I said if I didn't double check everything and the brewery fell on his head, it was his own fault."

Cecil Moncrieff's career had been undistinguished, his brewery design derided as unadventurous. But he seemed happy enough when we visited him at his offices, barely visible behind piles of plans.

"Creaser..." he said peevishly. "Asked for a modern brewery and then when I showed him the design, he picked up my pencil and scribbled all over it. I redrafted; he did it again. This carried on for weeks!"

"You hated him?" asked Holmes.

"It was tedious more than anything else. I was glad to see the back of him."

"Yet you still did a tour of the finished building?" said Holmes.

Moncrieff sat up.

"I wasn't going to let a troll like him prevent me. He said I was weak because I only designed the buildings, never 'got my hands dirty.' I don't see what's good about having dirty hands."

"Did you see anything that concerned you about the building?"

"It was passable work. Creaser of course had changed the purpose of some of the rooms, but I didn't care enough to want to get back in contact with that odious man."

Phyllis Tandforth was making an ornamental garden for a local Lord, and her rows of trees and flowers were somehow straighter than the walls of the brewery. She was in fact

building a wall as we walked up.

"Careful where you stand, gentlemen," she said brusquely. "Haven't yet laid the sub-base on that path."

Although she was an older lady, she seemed unaffected by the cold wind and rain.

"Like to do the work myself. Takes longer, but you can guarantee the craftsmanship," she said.

"I told Creaser the garden wouldn't be ready when the factory was, and he blew his top," she smiled.

"Mr. Gunter and Mr. Moncrieff both disliked Mr. Creaser too," said Holmes.

"Oh, I didn't dislike him! Reminded me of Pater. An objectionable old trout, a bit too fond of his own bitter. Gunter was always complaining about me as well; 'women' getting in the way. I never met Moncrieff."

She stood up on the wall she had finished, despite the mortar not yet being dry.

"If you don't mind, I've got a cart of compost on its way."

On the train back to Baker Street, Holmes seemed relaxed.

"In truth, I suspected the answer before I even met any of them," he said. "But I needed data. Mustn't build a sloppy case."

Question: Who does Sherlock Holmes suspect killed Creaser and walled up his body?

Hint: Quality.

15 The Red Right Hand

Mr. Necessiter's rooms looked like a museum of the maritime: walls covered with maps, tables full of navigational instruments. Necessiter's passion for the sea was, however, curtailed by seasickness.

He sadly indicated an empty case.

"Five years ago, I kept my twelfth-century Chinese compass there. I came home to find the door forced, the compass gone. The only clue, this red handprint."

He pointed at a large, clear red hand shape on the wall.

"A decorator left some red paint here. I thought it an accident, but the lid was on the tin."

Holmes measured the handprint and consulted his records.

"This right hand is the same size and shape of Hamish Strong's. A mariner I suspected of robbery seven years ago."

"I bought items from him in the past!" said Necessiter.

"There's your man," I said. "Caught red-handed."

Except: Hamish Strong told us that he had lost his right hand in an accident a year before the robbery!

"Crushed by a falling mast," Hamish said, waving his hook. "I don't know whose handprint that is, but it ain't mine. Unless it crawled away and took up burglary."

"That is definitely your hand," said Holmes. "We only have your word that the accident occurred before the robbery."

"Check the logbooks. Or ask my shipmates. One of them lives near here, Hugh Pattins, he works for that butcher."

"Allardyce's," said Holmes. "I helped him get that job. Anyone you think might want to incriminate you?"

"I've no real enemies," said Strong. "No real friends, either. Hold on... that artist... Luther Williams! He took a cast of my hand with rubber. Said he was collecting 'hands of the working man.' He's friends with Necessiter."

"Then it must be Williams," I declared.

"I did take a cast of Mr. Strong's hand," said Luther Williams, his garret filled with plaster casts of hands, feet, and faces. "But it was the left hand."

"Of course it was!" said Holmes. "You did not make a cast of his right hand as well?"

"Did Strong say I cast both his hands, or just one?" asked Williams.

We both knew the answer.

"I can show you the cast if you like."

He produced the rubber cast of Strong's left hand. Traces of plaster remained on its surface, and Holmes examined it with interest.

"You are friends with Tor Necessiter?" Holmes asked, using his magnifying glass to look closer.

"Oh, yes. Well, Tor is not really a 'friendly' person exactly, but he has great interest in any nautical art I own or create," said Williams. "We share a passion for the sea, even if I'm the only one who can actually bear to go sailing."

"And what do you think of Hamish Strong? Could he commit the robbery?"

"Oh, I hope not," said Luther with a smile. "Mariners can be very principled at sea and then suddenly when they're on land they find themselves adrift, as it were, and make bad decisions."

Our final suspect, Hugh Pattins, had made a good decision. Holmes had falsely advertised for the role of a harpooner to catch a murderer and Pattins had applied, getting a half-sovereign for his trouble, and when the butcher who had allowed Holmes to test harpoons on his meat told him customers had enjoyed the tenderized quality, Holmes had recommended Pattins for a job there.

"I likes it here greatly, Mr. Holmes," Pattins said enthusiastically, brushing his lank hair out of his eyes. "Boats is dangerous, and cold and wet. It's cold here too, especially the ice room, but the only wet is blood and the only danger is to the animals!"

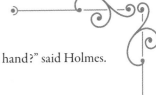

"Yes. Mr. Strong said you sailed with him on the voyage he lost his hand?" said Holmes.

Pattins thought hard. "Oh yes, I remember, a seal bit it off."

"He said the mast fell on it," I replied.

"Oh? Oh yes! The seal bit off Desmond O'Leary's toe, I think. Strong's hand was smashed. When the surgeon cut it off it looked so interesting, like a glove. I suppose my interest in meat started then," Pattin said, smiling. He stepped away from the cutting block, pulling his gloves off.

"And have you ever met Tor Necessiter? Or Luther Williams?" asked Holmes, examining the inverted gloves.

Pattin thought hard. "No. I knew a Muriel Necessary. Is he her brother?"

Back at Baker Street, Holmes examined some documents.

"The logbook does indeed confirm Strong's story. And when I asked him about the cast, he confirmed that it was of his left hand."

"What if..." I began, "...Pattins stole Strong's severed hand, and has kept it preserved somehow and used it to make the handprint!"

"Congratulations, Watson! You have somehow concocted a theory too ridiculous even for us. No, to find the solution to this case, you must consider the inverse of the evidence..."

Question: Who does Holmes suspect stole the compass and left the handprint?

Hint: Inverse.

16 The Character Assassin

Five years ago, Jason Reynolds' novels had caused controversy. They were roman à clefs, revealing scandalous things about real London citizens, politicians, and businessmen, all under the veil of false character names.

"Reynolds was found dead in the Thames two years later," said Holmes. "Misadventure, allegedly. It was 'common knowledge' he took opium. His body was emaciated, covered in sores. But due to his novels, everyone suspected murder... "

Before his death there were rumblings of libel, and afterward his publishers withdrew and pulped all the books.

"Why was the file in the Anathema Archive?" I asked.

"Shortly after Reynolds was found, Mars O'Malley had apparently skipped town," said Holmes.

O'Malley, a notorious tramp, fluctuated between drunken indigency and killing for money. He might have been hired to kill Reynolds and absconded with his pay.

Holmes sensed three people came out of his books worse than anyone.

The adulterous politician Lord Foolsbury was a clear caricature of Sir Philip Brule.

"Reynolds, that disgusting liar!" he spat. "I was going to sue him and that dratted publisher, but I held fire. Seems he got his just deserts."

"You suspected foul play?" asked Holmes.

"Nothing foul about it. It was opium, or a drunken brawl," Brule said.

"Weren't you Eton boxing champion twice?" said Holmes.

"I'll admit, I did entertain the thought of finding him and giving him a stout blow," said Brule. "But the coward always avoided any club or event I attended. Kept a low profile in general, no doubt to avoid offended parties like me."

Our second suspect was "Ma" Rose Berry, owner of a network of opium dens across

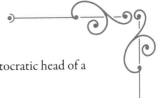

London. She appeared in Reynolds' books as Lady Violet Apricot, aristocratic head of a sprawling family whose activities mirrored her real-life empire.

She seemed amused by the whole thing.

"Kill 'im? I loved them books! Me, a lady?" she said, bursting into laughter.

"Didn't you worry about how accurate his depiction of your empire was?" asked Holmes.

"I won't lie, it did worry me. I reckoned he had an insider. But it didn't cause any problems. My rivals aren't big readers, and neither are the police. Most of it was common knowledge, none of my big secrets," she said.

"What about the disappearance of Mars O'Malley?" asked Holmes. "He's worked for you before."

"That sot worked for everyone. Always changing sides, always on the losing one somehow. Don't know how he got a reputation as a master killer; he was just a tramp, really. Underneath that massive beard he had the muscles of a chaffinch. Still, I hear Reynolds was a bony fellow as well, so maybe he could have done for him.

"Did Reynolds ever frequent any of your opium houses?" Holmes asked.

"If he did, it was under a false name, like in his books. Wish I'd met him, I'd have shaken his hand. Lady Apricot, ha!"

The final suspect was the publisher of the novels, Arnold Joynes. A broad-shouldered, broad-bellied man with wispy yellow hair.

"When Mr. Reynolds first approached me, I was uncertain," he said in a surprisingly light voice. "He seemed to come from nowhere, and the stories were shocking. But he reassured me that he had changed the names and details enough for us to be immune to persecution, so I took the risk. Wouldn't want to be engaged in a criminal enterprise."

Holmes declined to mention he knew Joynes had been briefly charged with forgery a decade ago.

"People were surprised you would publish novels that brutally criticized yourself," said Holmes.

The books contained a publisher named Arbuthnot Joyless, a cowardly, ugly, thick-witted man, constantly tricked by a handsome nameless author.

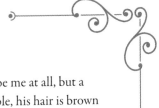

Joynes smiled and shook his head.

"Mr. Reynolds assured me that Arbuthnot Joyless is not meant to be me at all, but a composite of other publishers who rejected his manuscript. For example, his hair is brown and mine is fair. Also, his middle name is Keith and mine is Simon."

"Were you upset when he died?" Holmes asked.

"Oh, of course! I wouldn't say we were friends, but he didn't have many. I was forced to identify his body. He had documents on him that proved his identity, but they wanted to be sure. I wish I'd known he was taking opium; perhaps I could have helped. Stop it, I mean," he said, seemingly sad.

"Did you think he may have been killed?" asked Holmes.

"It crossed my mind, of course. Before his novels, we mostly published police almanacs. And some inspector came round asking me about some O'Malley person. But the coroner concluded it was drugs and drowning."

We left and Holmes seemed almost delighted.

"Such ingenuity wasted on such a pointless cause," he said.

Question: Who does Holmes suspect was responsible for the death of Jason Reynolds?

Hint: Existence.

⟨17⟩ The False Statue

We had journeyed to Bath, where there was a roving exhibition of historical art. Tapestries, paintings, mosaics, and the pièce de résistance, the Venus de Milo statue. There was no theft, but instead the opposite: an extra item had mysteriously appeared in the exhibition, a small, odd statue that was a mix of many media (wood, metal) and many cultures (Greek, Chinese).

"A visitor found it three weeks ago," said Holmes as we entered.

"And this case was already in the Anathema Archive?"

"The investigating officer was so baffled by this object that he immediately marked the file with an A and retired," he said, staring at the Venus de Milo with bafflement.

"It is bizarre," I agreed.

"It's not the only unexpected... addition to the art here," said Holmes cryptically.

The room's contents were personally guarded every night by the exhibition's overseer, Pierre Diderot, even though he had to sleep during the day. He was a suspect, as was the curator Horace Thigsby, and the resident docent, Nicole Montserrat.

"I attended the museum's connected art school," Miss Montserrat said. "Until I had financial difficulties."

"Did Mr. Thigsby hire you?" asked Holmes.

"Yes, said he wanted someone who knew the art, but I suspect he chose me for my face. He clearly doesn't care for anything I say... "

"Is Monsieur Diderot the same?"

"I have barely met him," she said. "He sleeps all day in a room at my boarding house. Such a loud snorer."

"What do you make of the object?" said Holmes.

"It's a cobbled-together lump of nonsense. It has distracted everyone. I wonder if that is the point."

"I wondered that too," said Holmes. "Have you noticed anything odd about the other artworks?"

"That side of things is out of my hands, m'sieur," she said.

Horace Thigsby had an air of authority, but seemed far out of his depth.

"It was a great privilege for our institution to host this exhibition, and this strange incident could detract from that!" he said.

"Why do you think it appeared?" asked Holmes.

"I think that Diderot chap has hit on a scheme," said Thigsby. "We only have his word that this is not an authentic part of the exhibition. He alters the records, claims it isn't real, and then can sell it on for his own profit!"

"A very clever ruse," said Holmes sardonically. "The only thing standing in his way is that the inventory of the exhibition has been well documented during the several years it has been visiting cities across the world, and that the object is clearly not of any real antiquity."

"Yes, well," said Thigsby. "You should interrogate him nonetheless."

"What about Miss Montserrat?" asked Holmes.

"Her?" Thigsby laughed. "Mr. Holmes, you need not concern yourself. She is an... ornament, shall we say. I felt the exhibition needed an extra element to draw in the crowds and I noticed her beauty."

"But she has knowledge of art and culture?"

Thigsby rolled his eyes. "A parrot may be taught to talk, but that does not make it a lecturer. She is just like the Venus de Milo over there, beautiful but inert. In fact, there is quite a resemblance, especially the arms and hands. They are delicate but strong," Thigsby said, before suddenly blushing, aware he'd said too much.

Pierre Diderot seemed a little bleary but was passionate.

"You have no idea how much I feared that something would be stolen!" he said. "When the Louvre tasked me with this touring exhibition, I felt both blessed and cursed. How

could I trust a mere security guard of each country to defend these priceless artefacts? So, when it was found that their number had not dwindled but multiplied, well, I was baffled!"

"Are you sure you did not see or hear anything that night?"

Diderot looked a little ashamed. "I will be honest m'sieur, even though I have kept this nocturnal schedule for about 17 months, I have somehow still not adapted, and will on occasion fall asleep."

"I would also intuit that sleep deprivation may have blunted your faculties of observation somewhat," said Holmes, looking around the room.

"Not so, sir! I have observed that Thigsby covets the collection. Perhaps he means to discredit me and secure it here permanently. And Miss Montserrat has woken me several times during the day in the boarding house. Supposedly to halt my 'snoring,' but I suspect she holds hostile views toward the Louvre. Perhaps they refused to teach her."

"And what do you make of the object?" Holmes asked.

"It means nothing to me. Some kind of joke," said Diderot, yawning.

"What about the other artworks?"

"I don't know what to make of it, Holmes," I said afterward.

"The case or the object?" he asked.

"Both! It all seems ridiculous."

"Yes, but in fact a serious crime has been committed here, whether for profit or
mischief I'm not yet sure. But the culprit is ironically just about to run into the long arm of the law..."

Question: Who does Holmes think planted the strange statue in the exhibition and why?

Hint: Arms.

18 The Accidental Burglar

Arnold Jones had apparently burst into a police station and confessed to his role in a heist.

"After my inheritance, I moved here for some peace and quiet," he said. "I didn't realize how rowdy London was. Next door, the Elsinore Club was noisy; they were often breaking things. No better than criminals. I was worried about burglars, I wanted a safe, and I saw a newspaper advertisement for what I thought to be a 'safe-picking' course. I arrived at this small room where there were two suspicious looking individuals...

- "Big John," a tall, rotund individual in bright clothes, face barely visible behind a huge beard.
- "The Hunchback," a stooped man in furs with a broad-brimmed hat and goggles.

"I was too scared to leave. It wasn't a lecture; instead, they had me work the tumblers of a safe. They thought I was a 'safe cracker.' I must have a knack for it because I was bundled into a carriage and taken to the shop of some costermonger named Guildenstern. They gruffly told me he had a safe filled with jewels!" he said.

"It was pitch dark, they smashed the window, then pushed me into this large room, empty but for the safe. I opened it and jewels tumbled out! They scooped them up and pushed me out, dropped me back outside my house with a handful of jewels, and said to 'keep my trap shut.'"

"And the jewels?" asked Holmes.

"Threw them down the sewer. Wish I hadn't; when I went to the police station, they didn't believe me."

"They investigated?" I said.

"Days later, a constable came to say two criminals had been caught. He said Guildenstern wouldn't press charges; I should forget about it. A month later, I saw Big

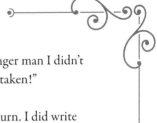

John! He'd lost weight and shaved, but it was him, walking with a younger man I didn't know, medium height, sandy hair. I told the police; they said I was mistaken!"

"Do you have any enemies?" asked Holmes.

"Guildenstern? And this Constable Kite seemed annoyed at my return. I did write several letters of complaint to the Elsinore Club; I doubt they liked me."

We visited the now Sergeant Kite. He was medium height, and I noticed some silvery-sandy hair under his hat.

"I buried the file," he said shortly. "Unfair a law-abiding man like Mr. Jones would face charges."

"How were Big John and The Hunchback captured?" asked Holmes.

"Wasn't told the details. Just that they were," he said tersely.

"Why didn't Mr. Guildenstern prosecute Mr. Jones?" asked Holmes.

"I can't talk about this," Kite whispered. "There's been threats to my li... No one was harmed!"

Kite wouldn't be drawn on it further.

We found no details for Oscar Guildenstern, so we visited the address from the file, near Covent Garden. It was a dress shop run by a middle-aged woman named Gertrude Long. She was tall and she wore her blonde hair in a bun.

"Did you know Guildenstern, the former owner?" I asked.

She shook her head.

"Who am I, Rosencrantz? The landlord's always been Mr. Grundy."

"Guildenstern was a costermonger here, eight years ago."

"No, he wasn't," she said. "I've been here for 14 years."

"Do you have a backroom?" asked Holmes. "With a safe?"

"My backroom's filled with rolls of fabric," she said.

We inspected the room and found it small, with no window.

"Watson, either the wrong address was appended to the file, or every speck of Mr. Guildenstern has been removed," said Holmes.

The Elsinore Club was for wealthy young men to cause mischief before getting high-

paying jobs. Disbanded two years previously, we met with a Lord Tristram Meriwether MP, former member, and cabinet official.

"Old Mr. Jones!" he said. "Spent so much time calling us criminals, now you say he was a jewel thief?"

Meriwether listened to the case's details, looking delighted. When we had finished, he affected a more sober expression.

"I hope you're not accusing me of criminal connections..."

"No. But your club's treasurer, Finian Procter, did go to jail last year for embezzlement," said Holmes.

"Shouldn't you speak to him, then?" said Meriwether gruffly.

"I just wondered if you had witnessed anything untoward," said Holmes.

"The club wasn't debauched," Meriwether said defensively. "We studied Shakespeare. *Hamlet*, *Richard III*, *The Merry Wives of Windsor*... It was more about performances, dressing up and... pranks," said Meriwether.

"I meant the general vicinity," said Holmes. "They dropped him outside his house."

"No. Sounds like he had a lucky escape," said Meriwether, who had slumped down in his chair like a naughty schoolboy.

As we left, Holmes was almost chuckling to himself.

"Watson, the identity of our third man is clear. Even if, in fact, he wasn't a third man at all."

Question: Who was the "third man" witnessed walking with Big John?

Hint: Revenge.

19 The Disappearing Roofer

"How does a man disappear in mid-air?" asked Godfrey Vranch.

Holmes entreated Mr. Vranch to tell the story.

"I was a roofer. Me, Harold Stiles, and Maynard Proops. Good workers, though Proops was a bit of a Casanova. Three years ago, we were working on this inn in Cornwall, fixing it up for the new landlady. The inn was too close to the road, shook every time people thundered past. Speaking of thunder, a great storm started. Stiles shouted to Proops, 'Get off the roof!' Lightning, you see. Proops said he wanted to finish the spars; told Stiles to throw him his hammer."

"Stiles could throw a hammer onto a roof?" I asked.

"Arm like a locomotive. I knew Proops had been seeing Stiles' wife, and I think Stiles knew too because he slung his hammer like a horseshoe. Proops catches it but he's unbalanced, there's a deafening clap of thunder… and he falls backward off the roof! We ran round to the front of the house and… nothing. Proops had vanished."

The landlady, Enid Lawrence, was inside the house and said she saw him fall past the window. But Walter Mochrie, a farmer riding past on his cart, said he hadn't seen anyone falling at all.

Harold Stiles still worked as a roofer. He wouldn't come down from the roof he was repairing, so Holmes and I ascended.

"Wasn't trying to hurt him," he said. "He wanted a hammer, he got a hammer."

"Did you suspect him and your wife of…" said Holmes.

Stiles turned to him with his eyes blazing.

"It wasn't much of a secret. But work is work. We had a job to do, and I wanted to get it done. I was going to wring his neck once we were finished," he said bitterly. "Then he vanished."

"How long did it take to run around to the house's front?" asked Holmes.

"A minute? There were big piles of materials either side. Not enough time to go in a window. The landlady would have seen him."

"Unless she was helping," Holmes said.

"She had no time for his nonsense," Stiles said. "The way he fell, he'd have to be a bloody vampire to hang on!"

Enid Lawrence was a solid old lady with little time for fancies. She still ran the inn, Hope House.

"I already told the police. I hired them to repair the roof. Doing a passable job. I'm inside the house repairing a wall and a storm picks up, wind rattling the frames. I hear shouting and banging, and then there's this crack of thunder and one of them flies past the window. I run down and there's the other two standing there like stunned sheep. But no dead man. And trust me, he would have been dead; you don't fall that far and live."

"Could they have dragged his body off somewhere?" I asked.

"No time, I was down in 20 seconds. One of them went to get the police and I watched the other one until they arrived, and they searched everywhere, inside, outside, in all the boxes."

"What about the farmer, Walter Mochrie? Did you see him and his cart?" asked Holmes.

"No. I know him, his farm is opposite here, up the hill. Always reckless with his cart. But when I came down, I was occupied looking for this roofer in the wind and rain. It was the police who got a statement from him."

"So, what do you think happened to him?" I asked.

She shrugged. "Maybe he blew away. Now do you want a room or not?"

Walter Mochrie was somehow even more taciturn than Mrs. Lawrence, his thin, stony face gazing over the yard of his farm.

"They asked what I saw so I told them. Nothing," he muttered.

"But you were definitely looking at the roof of the house at the time in question?" asked Holmes.

"Aye. They were doing a poor job. Roof like that might last in the town, but countryside, another question. Stronger winds, stronger rain. I could see Lawrence in the

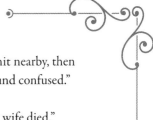

window, then there's this clap of thunder. I turn to see if lightning has hit nearby, then when I looked back, they were coming round the side and looking around confused."

"I see. And you were riding your haycart at the time?"

"Yes. Heading into town to get provisions. Just me up here after my wife died."

"Mrs. Lawrence said you tend to drive your haycart like a phaeton. Are you sure you were able to see what you said?" asked Holmes.

"There's nothing wrong with my eyesight, Mr. Holmes," Mochrie replied. "I can see a good deal better than her."

"Yes, indeed," said Holmes afterward. "He can see a good deal. And so can I. I can see what happened to Maynard Proops, at least."

Question: Who does Sherlock Holmes suspect is responsible for the disappearance of Maynard Proops?

Hint: Road.

20 The Beastly Lair

Four years ago, Duncan Murray moved from Edinburgh to the small town of Invercree to work as notary for the mayor.

"The locals were sullen and hostile," Murray said. "Then my boarding house's landlady said that a warlock lived there!"

"The infamous 'Judas Mallifer,'" said Holmes.

"The job was fine, but I dreaded walking through the streets," he said. "The house opposite was even occupied by a Canadian fur trapper who sought 'rare skins.' Two months after arriving, I found myself lost in a mist. I turned a corner and witnessed a horrifying tableau. A red-lit room, wall hung with the furred skins of some limbless creature. Within, a bald figure crouched, face twisted in malice, and a small hairy creature, bowed, presenting it with a pelt."

"What did you do?"

"I stumbled backward into a dustbin. At the sound, the bald one's furious eyes turned to me. A third, unseen figure in the room suddenly burst from a door in pursuit. I turned and ran but felt a strike on the back of my head..."

He grimaced at the memory.

"I awoke in my bed. The police thought I had been drinking. I searched during the daytime but never found the lair. So, I tendered my resignation and returned to Edinburgh."

"Do you think he was inebriated?" I asked Holmes after Murray had left.

"Only on fear, perhaps," said Holmes.

We made the journey to Invercree, which was much more charming than Mr. Murray suggested.

"He had a delicate constitution," said John Fairbairn, the town's mayor. Despite being in his sixties, he seemed remarkably healthy, with a thick head of black hair.

"We did our best to welcome him here. I fear the local whisky was too strong for him."

"He is a teetotaller," said Holmes.

"So he says. And this story about a bogeyman killing animals. More likely he saw a butcher, or a tanner."

"Mr. Murray insisted it was neither of those places," said Holmes. "Was he a good worker?"

"Adequate, but slow," he said. "I insist my employees move and think fast. That's what my father taught me," he said, gesturing to the portrait of his patriarch at age 25, in his role as the previous mayor. Their eyes had the same mischievous twinkle, even if the hairline was much higher and thinner.

"What about the local warlock, or the fur trapper?" asked Holmes.

"I doubt either had any hand in this. Mallifer is a cackling old imbecile, and Leclerc is fine... for a Frenchman."

Edouard Leclerc did not dress in the manner you might expect a fur trapper would, wearing a well-cut tweed suit, but he did insist on wearing a huge beaver-skin hat indoors, which lent him an air of ridiculousness.

"I met this Murray only once," Leclerc said. "I told him I came to catch the blue-throated pine marten."

"Have you caught it?" asked Holmes.

"Sadly not. The creature is elusive. The people here are surprisingly noisy," he said unhappily.

"Like Murray?" Holmes asked.

"I mean that preening mayor, or the supposed wizard, but I would hear Murray cry out occasionally," Leclerc said.

"What do you think he saw?" Holmes asked.

"I don't display my furs like paintings," Leclerc said. "It must have been a shop."

He pulled off his fur hat and fanned himself with it. Holmes and I took careful note of his hair, long on the sides but thinning on top...

Judas Mallifer's rooms were a maze of occult bric-à-brac. A spry old man, he sat in a black chair and grinned maliciously at Holmes and I, light glinting off his pale bald head.

"I assure you I had no involvement in Mr. Murray's incident," he said with wicked glee.

"We won't bother you further," said Holmes, gathering his coat. Mallifer looked disappointed.

"How is your brother, by the way?" he said sardonically.

Holmes was suddenly the angriest I had seen him in years, and in one swift move had his hand inches away from Mallifer's face, showing him a photograph.

"Watch your words carefully, Sidney Boggins," Holmes hissed. "You are no more an intelligencer than you are a warlock. Whatever you think you know through your connections is nothing. Tell me everything you know about this case."

Mallifer was white as a sheet and any pretence of menace had departed him entirely.

"Th-the mayor's a fool; only got the job because of his father. Incredibly vain."

"He thinks poorly of you as well," said Holmes acidly.

"He's frightened of me; we've had a few hair-raising encounters. Ironic, really..."

"What of Leclerc?" snapped Holmes.

"The trapper's a smuggler, wouldn't know a pine marten if it bit him on the nose. I'd bet sixpence that fur hat is the only fur he even owns," Mallifer said bitterly.

"Thank you for your assistance, Mr. Boggins," Holmes said archly.

"I suppose we had better look for this 'lair' now," I said.

"No need, I know exactly where and what it is and see no need to bother the owner, or his no doubt publicity-shy patrons..." said Holmes, smiling.

Question: Who does Holmes suspect of being the figure in the "lair?"

Hint: Hair.

21 The Fiery Phoenix

Nine years ago, the offices of *Palimpsest*, an anarchist newspaper, burned to a cinder before the publication of its 11th issue. The investigating officer, no fan of anarchism, happily sent its file off to the Anathema Archive. Holmes suspected Mr. Threlfall, an arsonist for hire who had found religion while in jail.

"That was my fire. Why do ye care for those heathens?" Threlfall said.

"Others in the building might have died," said Holmes.

"Never! My fires are carefully contained," he objected.

"Did you burn their offices out of protest?"

"I never set a fire for free," he said, annoyed.

"Then who hired you?" asked Holmes.

Threlfall mimed locking his lips.

Holmes had three suspects. Did Percival Rooker, the newspaper's proprietor, seek an insurance payout? Or might Desdemona Smythe, the landlady, want to get rid of a problem tenant? Or perhaps the occupant next door, the elderly doll-maker, Mary Haskin, had objected to Rooker's presence?

Rooker now published a similar paper called the *Phoenix*, from a house in Guildford.

"Why burn my own property?" asked Rooker. "I'm sure your investigations showed I had no insurance."

"True," said Holmes. "But there are other financial incentives. The name *Phoenix* suggests a righteous resurrection..."

Rooker shrugged. "My cause needs as much assistance as it can get."

"Your landlady received insurance money. She didn't share the spoils?" asked Holmes.

"I didn't ask. We are old friends, and while Desdemona supports the cause, I always aim to protect her. So, after the fire I left her building," he said.

"What about Mary Haskin, who lived next door? Did she object to your activities?"

"Trust me, she is no doll-maker. Her flat was constantly filled with sweatshop workers. Poor, exploited people, the kind we are trying to help."

"Mrs. Smythe didn't object?" Holmes asked.

"She believed Haskin's little old lady routine. She came to her senses when I published an article about it in the 10th issue," he said.

Desdemona Smythe had inherited her wealth from her father and was surprisingly forthright for a woman. Her office had a Roman feel, with white columns, mosaics, and statues.

"I have a lot of residences, so I was not in a position to personally check whether Mrs. Haskin was misusing Flat 2," she said defensively. "After the fire, I visited, and upon finding evidence, I evicted her immediately. I don't run a rookery!"

"Some may disagree, considering the subversive content of Mr. Rooker's paper," said Holmes.

"I don't find it subversive," Mrs. Smythe said. "The corruption of our government is much worse. Their 'democracy' bears as much resemblance to the Roman Republic as a trough of pigs."

"You don't think that Mr. Rooker would resort to violent tactics?" asked Holmes.

Desdemona laughed. "Percy would faint if he even knocked over a candle by accident!"

Mary Haskin did indeed seem an almost perfect facsimile of a sweet little old lady, and I could tell that Holmes was immediately both impressed and repulsed. She was now supposedly the proprietor of a doily store.

"Oh my, yes, that was a frightening day!" she said, eyes wide. "I had just finished putting eyes into little Elsie Grey when I smelled this terrible smoke. Luckily I had the side door open for some fresh air and was able to walk out that way. Mrs. Smythe's fire escape might have been poorly built, but it did indeed work."

"Yes," said Holmes. "And there was no one else in your flat at this time?"

"Well..." she said coyly, "there was Elsie Grey, and Lizbeth, and sweet little Dot, and all the other little dollies that I make."

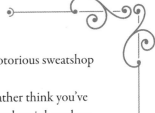

"I see. What if I were to suggest that you are in fact Mary Shank, notorious sweatshop scurf?"

She pantomimed shock. "Mr. Holmes, what an odd suggestion. I rather think you've got the wrong end of the stick. It was that Mr. Rooker who was a criminal, a violent thug looking to murder businessmen and politicians. And that Smythe woman, I heard tell she had her fingers in many illicit pies."

"Tell among whom, the doll-making community?" I queried.

"She tried to make me leave, no doubt to install some more bomb-chucking communards, but I held firm despite her lies," she said, and then claimed she was tired and would close the shop.

"She's definitely Shank," Holmes said as we walked to the building. "She was very afraid we would want to see what was in the back of her doily shop. But she's not wrong about Mrs. Smythe either; she has some rather seedy connections."

The relevant floor of the building had not been repaired since the fire, but simply blocked off. It had the same Roman flair as Desdemona's office, right down to Roman numerals for the flat numbers. Holmes entered but seemed uninterested in the burned shell of Flat 3, instead picking up a metal shape from the ground.

"An I," Holmes said. "This explains everything."

Question: Who does Sherlock Holmes suspect hired Mr. Threlfall?

Hint: Roman.

22 The Dark Tower

We had come to the Wrecker's Inn in the village of Greye, on the Kent coast. One hundred years ago, this area was notorious for its smuggling, but all it had to merit it now was a handsome lighthouse and the idea that, five years previously, a supernatural event had occurred.

"Some think I'm a pirate," Roland Beukes said, pointing at his eyepatch. "The truth is I was an iron monger, lost my eye to molten metal. Wouldn't know a boat from a bucket. When I lost my job I had to come to Kent, help out at my sister's inn."

A month later, he was heading back alone to the inn from the lighthouse, where he would sometimes drink with the keeper, Harney Barlow.

"Moon was so full I didn't need a lamp. Walking along the coastal path I heard a crashing sound and suddenly this great dark tower rose up on my right! Far away, just growing out of the ground. About a mile tall, jet-black, no windows, two gatherings of spikes on either side. Suddenly the ground shook and I fell backward, cracked my head on a stone. When I awoke, the sun was up and the tower had gone. And so had Harney."

The lighthouse keeper had disappeared. Beukes told the police.

"They said I'd just seen the lighthouse. But I was coming from there!" he said.

"Did the keeper have any other friends?" asked Holmes.

"He was solitary, but there was three others he'd see."

First was the inn's landlady, Roland's sister Marjory. She believed her brother.

"Roland's not a tale-teller or drunkard," Marjory said. "When he told me of the dark tower, I believed it. Strange things happen round here, like the black dog. A dark tower was new to me. Until I heard that poem."

"By Robert Browning?" asked Holmes.

"The man who read it was called Tristram Black. A week after the encounter, he read it out

loud in the inn. All about this dark tower; at the end he says Roland and I practically fainted. I marched over thinking he'd used my brother's story, and he tells me the poem was written 40 years ago by someone else. 'Coincidence!' Turns out he was the new lighthouse keeper."

"What about Harney Barlow?" said Holmes.

"Came in for a drink sometimes, talk only to Roland. He went to church regularly; he didn't seem like the type. I suppose Reverend Cooper must welcome everyone. Mr. Black is more sociable, but I won't have him in here!"

Tristram Black was surprisingly well educated.

"When I took over it was a mess. Barlow had little interest in keeping things shipshape," Mr. Black said.

"You read Browning's poem in the inn?" said Holmes.

"I'm trying to be a poet," said Black. "Took this job hoping the isolation might help. I thought I could see if any locals shared my passion, so I did an impromptu reading of the Browning. Then the landlady charged over accusing me of witchcraft! She probably did me a kindness barring me."

"Have you met Roland Beukes?" asked Holmes.

"I've steered clear, out of fear of his sister."

"What about Reverend Cooper?"

"Just once. I know I should attend church, but I don't want to get caught up in local business. He came round seeing if I was interested in joining his flock, but left me alone when he found out that I'm not poor."

"What do you think Roland's dark tower was?" asked Holmes.

"I should be poetic... but I think it was probably just a tree," Black said.

Reverend Aaron Cooper was a grizzled old man with a weather-beaten face. Most people would peg Black for the vicar and Cooper for the lighthouse keeper.

"Bunch of heathens round here," he spat. "Few come to services. I try, but they would rather go to that inn."

"How did you move from being a mariner to a vicar?" asked Holmes.

"How did you... yes, I was a sailor, but 20 years hence one close shave too many brought

me to the Lord," he said.

"You sought out a parish near the sea?" asked Holmes.

"I might have little flock, but the waves remind me of my promise. And the lighthouse's light of my duty."

"You were friends with the lighthouse keeper?"

"No, he came to me for confession, but I was not his kind of company. That was Roland Beukes. A man who, when his only friend fails in his responsibility and runs away, makes up a story about some tower!" Cooper shouted.

"You think it was a lie?" asked Holmes.

"Yes, though the dark tower he invented does resemble a cross," he said.

As we left, Holmes peered at the lighthouse, shining brightly in the dark.

"I think I see the light. Remember this area's history, and that Roland has only one eye..."

Question: Who does Holmes suspect was responsible for Harney Barlow's disappearance?

Hint: Boats.

23 The Perfect Disguise

I was dining with Holmes and Watson at 221b Baker Street. We each enjoyed a plate of Mrs. Hudson's excellent mutton while Holmes examined one of the Archive's files, the tale of a disappearance in a cornfield.

"Hopkins…" Holmes began, "it is clear the farmer's brother disguised himself crouched among the sheaves and was the supposed drifter the farmer forced off his land."

"Impossible!" I said. "He stood inches away, even grabbed his shirt. He would recognize his own brother, no matter how good the disguise."

"Hopkins, Holmes has on occasion worn a disguise so cunning even I did not recognize him!" replied Watson.

"I propose a challenge," Holmes declared. "You shall meet with a few people and one will be myself, in disguise. If you can tell which is me, I'll accept your point."

Sure enough, roughly 48 hours later I received a message asking me to return to Baker Street at 7 pm. On arrival Dr. Watson let me in, an uncharacteristically mischievous gleam in his eye.

"Good luck, old fellow," he said, stroking his moustache. "I would say he'll be right under your nose, but I rather think you knew that."

Sitting in the room were:

- An old man, practically skin and bones, in a tight black suit.
- A battle-worn but smiling soldier in civvies, missing an arm and a leg.
- A 10-year-old boy in worn work clothes and cloth cap, one of Holmes' infamous Baker Street Irregulars.

"This is Mr. Phineas Crelbourn, Sergeant Mick Ormerod, and Master Henry Ashwood," said Watson. "You have 10 minutes to question and observe them. I guarantee Sherlock Holmes is in this room!"

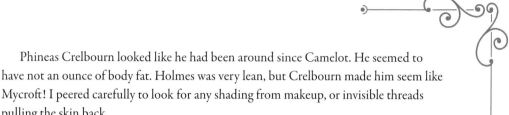

Phineas Crelbourn looked like he had been around since Camelot. He seemed to have not an ounce of body fat. Holmes was very lean, but Crelbourn made him seem like Mycroft! I peered carefully to look for any shading from makeup, or invisible threads pulling the skin back.

"Easy, young'un!" Crelbourn exclaimed. "I know Mister 'Olmes said we was to let you have a good look, but I ain't a waxwork."

"How do you know Holmes?" I asked.

"'E saved my life, but more importantly, my cart. I've been collecting rag and bone in Stepney since King William filled the throne. One day some blighter grabs the reins of my cart, makes to push me under the wheels. Turns out Mr. Holmes was hiding under some animal skins, and he stops this bloke straight off!"

"Can I see if your beard is glued on?" I asked.

"Glued? Glued?" he said, finding this hilarious. He began the driest laugh I've ever heard, like the wheezing of a church organ filled with sand, and then started choking on his own wit. I looked to Dr. Watson who hesitated, then surged forward and helped Crelbourn recover with stout pats on the back. I examined his beard, and it looked as real as any.

I next spoke to the supposed Sergeant Ormerod.

"You'll be wanting to check my arm and leg, won't you," he said cheerily. "It'll cost you! Guess how much?"

"An arm and a leg?" I said wearily.

"That's right!" he said, chuckling. I quickly began examining him before Crelbourn could start laughing at Ormerod's joke. He really seemed to have two missing limbs.

"It was a hell of a battle. Dr. Watson will attest, he was there," said Crelbourn, looking to the back of the room, then quickly to the window where Watson stood smiling. "I cursed the surgeon as he amputated them, but he saved my life, I'm sure."

"So, you know Watson, but not Holmes?" I asked, trying to see if his moustache was false.

"Oh, Mr. Holmes saved my life too! See, there was this trained kestrel..."

Ormerod's elaborate story of Holmes' kindness was absurd, but also entirely in keeping with the rest of his adventures. I could detect no falsity in his accent, his appearance, or story.

I almost considered not questioning or examining "Henry Ashwood" at all. Even Sherlock Holmes could not affect such a transformation.

Or could he? Maybe he had used some kind of perspective trick? Or maybe his legs were half hidden in some kind of trapdoor in the floor with false shoes applied to his knees.

"I'll dance if you want, mate!" Ashwood said chirpily, leaping up and performing a jig on the spot that put paid to my theory. I swear I could hear a muffled chuckle from the back of the room, but neither Crelbourn, Ormerod, nor Watson were laughing.

"This is the easiest money I've ever made," said Ashwood. "Half the time Mr. Holmes has had us shinnying up drainpipes or following sinister people for hours."

He could not have been Holmes. His frame was exactly that of a child. But then neither could Ormerod, or Crelbourn. Yet my 10 minutes were up, and I had to choose...

Question: Who does Inspector Hopkins suspect is Sherlock Holmes?

Hint: Four options.

24   The Bayswater Butcher

The Bayswater Butcher was one of the most mysterious criminal figures in London. His identity and even his occupation were closely guarded by the entire underworld: the lowliest pickpocket would rather be jailed for life than utter a word.

They were all terrified of him as well. Violent thugs went white when he was mentioned. "No one wants to see him," they'd say. "But everyone needs him."

But Holmes had found a file in the Archive which included a transcribed conversation with Sebastian Moran, Moriarty's chosen assassin.

Moran had drunkenly said he had reluctantly visited the Butcher. Yes, even "Tiger" Moran was petrified of them. He did not elaborate, but he mentioned three Bayswater residents.

First, Mr. Octavius Slate, owner of "Slate & Co" Milliners. The shop had little trade, so Holmes suspected it was a front for Moriarty's empire. He also felt Slate's appearance and manner was that of a master assassin, admitting that "some kind fellows are born with the physiology of an absolute fiend."

Slate's eyes, so pale as to almost look white, had an intense penetrating ferocity that you would not usually seek in a shop assistant, paired with his remarkable height and sallow face.

"'Bayswater Butcher?'" Slate said in a voice like a knife across a gravestone. "This is a hat shop."

"You cannot pretend you have never heard of the legend, Mr. Slate," said Holmes.

"I assure you I have no idea of what you are talking about," Slate intoned.

"Did Colonel Moran buy a hat here?" asked Holmes.

"Possibly," said Slate. "I don't have a good memory for faces. Only hats."

I picked up one of the hats and noticed that the price was twice that of his competitors. The quality was incredible, though. I almost bought it.

Our second destination was an actual butcher shop, owned by Leonard Bean, a short man with a neat moustache. He was in his back room cutting some beef with a scalpel.

"Some customers want a very slim cut of meat," he remarked. "The Bayswater Butcher? I fancy you mean that myth."

He wiped off the scalpel and put it in a leather bag.

"You have criminal connections?" I said accusingly.

"I daresay anyone who operates in Bayswater has some contact with criminals," said Holmes.

"Just so. They're often around here trying to sell me chickens they 'found' or offering discount equipment. I won't associate with that sort, and I only use quality tools," he said, gesturing toward some cleavers, syringes, and a stethoscope in the corner.

Bean did not seem a threatening figure at all; in fact, I felt a strange kinship with him. He did seem more well spoken than your average butcher.

"Do you recall Colonel Moran coming here?" asked Holmes.

"Oh, yes," said Bean, smiling. "He visited a few times asking about exotic meats. Caribou, antelope, even suggested I get some tiger steaks! I always told him to try the markets."

Our third destination was the house of Lady Hyacinth D'August, a wealthy widow and society fixture.

"Moran? Oh, you mean Basher!" she declared with delight from a small nest of crinoline. "Such a lovely fellow, always has an interesting story and such a charming way."

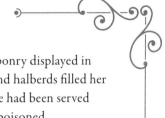

I was distracted from her testimony by the vast amounts of weaponry displayed in her house. Her walls were crammed with swords and rifles, spears and halberds filled her umbrella stand, and Holmes whispered to me that he was certain we had been served Earl Grey from an assassin's teapot, though he assured me it wasn't poisoned.

"You have rather a lot of... instruments of death," Holmes said, sounding almost impressed.

"Oh, those! They belonged to my late husband. Dear Samuel had such a penchant for those things," she tittered.

"But your husband died 18 years ago, and yet I am sure that rifle was only created seven years ago," said Holmes.

"Oh, well after he passed, I'll admit I have continued adding to his collection," Lady D'August said without a hint of guilt. "I suppose I don't like to admit to it as it's not very ladylike."

"And is that why the Colonel visited? To borrow something?" asked Holmes.

"Oh, don't be silly. These have all been rendered harmless," she said, getting a blunderbuss down and showing how the firing pin was missing. "No, he came to try and sell me some of his old guns, but he didn't have anything I didn't already own."

Back at Baker Street, Holmes was pensive. "I cannot reckon it. By my own analysis all three of them are essentially harmless, even if Mr. Slate projects an air of danger. So how can one of them be so feared by criminals, and yet protected?"

I smiled. "For once, Holmes, I think I may have the answer to this one. In fairness, it is my area of expertise..."

Question: Who does Dr. Watson suspect is the Bayswater Butcher?

Hint: Scalpel.

25 The Hidden Riches

Ten years ago, someone walked into Winchester bank, directly through to the vault, picked up a box full of gold sovereigns and walked out again. Only once the box was found to be missing did employees remember someone walking past them. They offered no description, and there was seemingly no evidence left.

Holmes took samples of dust from a box that had been next to the box, and we suddenly had three suspects.

"The sawdust is from the Arran whitebeam tree, extremely rare. Eight years ago, a furniture company in Winchester made chairs from it, with three employees," Holmes told me. "I have acquired their details. None of them were bank customers. Ten years with a fortune in sovereigns, I think it unlikely our criminal would not have spent any of it."

Edwin North now lived in a mansion on the outskirts of the city. His butler showed us into his drawing room, passing his employer a cigar.

"I heard about the robbery," he said. "I remember thinking we could have done with some of that ourselves. No one wanted the chairs."

"You have done well since," said Holmes.

"Inheritance from my aunt," North said. "She had no children. You can check with my lawyer."

"You're prepared," Holmes observed.

"You called ahead. Also, when I got the money, I left the business, and my partners sued me. They wanted a piece of my inheritance," said Mr. North.

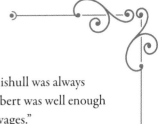

"Anything suspicious about your co-workers?" Holmes asked.

"I regret ever associating with either of them," said Mr. North. "Chishull was always looking down his nose at me, when I knew he was a potter's son. Cuthbert was well enough when he was off the gin, but he was always drunk, gambling away his wages."

Holmes' contacts confirmed North's inheritance story was allegedly true.

John Chishull was working as a waiter at a salubrious new restaurant in town, The Versailles. It was busy and the maître d', a sour-faced old gent, pointed at a younger man with a fashionable haircut carrying a tray.

"I can't speak long," Mr. Chishull said, glancing at the maître d'. "If I slow down, they'll sack me."

Holmes felt the dining room too noisy to talk, persuading the maître d' to allow us to speak to Chishull in an adjoining room.

"Now I'm glad you came," said Chishull in a croaky voice. "Five minutes' rest during the busy period!" His eyes darted toward the maître d' hovering nearby.

"How long have you worked here?" Holmes asked.

"Since it opened, seven years ago. Things went sour with the chair business; the others blamed me because it was my idea. It was their work that was shoddy!" Chishull said, before coughing.

The maître d' put a glass of water next to him, then picked it up again and left the room.

"North got that money from his aunt and didn't have the decency to invest," Chishull said. "We had to close, and I've had this job since."

"Mr. North said Mr. Cook had a gambling problem," said Holmes.

"Not as much now, but that's only because every bookmaker in the city refuses to take his bets," Chishull said. "If he left the city, he'll be back to it. Now I have to get back to work."

Cuthbert Cook was in a public house propping up the bar, arguing with the landlord about an unpaid tab. His cheery manner barely disguised his clear discomfort at our questioning.

"Robbery? Me? No!" he said grinning. "I'm the one being robbed, all the time, by slow horses, lame greyhounds, punch-drunk boxers..."

"I was told that you have been banned from betting in the area," said Holmes.

"Recently, yes," said Cook. "It's a conspiracy. As soon as my luck began to turn, the doors all slammed down. Can't have that, can they?"

"If we spoke to these bookmakers, how much money would you say you have lost? A small fortune?" asked Holmes.

"I see what you're getting at..." Cook said carefully. "But the fact is I've only ever gambled my wages. You wouldn't get the truth from those bookies anyway. You should check out Mr. La-di-da North, suddenly rich from some aunt I never heard of. Neither him nor Chishull would ever lend me a penny, even after I worked my fingers to the bone on those stupid chairs."

"And what do you do now?" Holmes asked, although he probably already knew from some stain on Cook's jacket.

"I survive," Cook said cagily.

From the pub we headed straight for the police station.

"A simple mistake immediately showed me the truth," said Holmes. "But not one made by one of our suspects."

Question: Who does Sherlock Holmes suspect committed the robbery?

Hint: Water.

26 The Watch in the Well

It was front page news: "Industrialist Phineas Arrow accidentally drowns in his own well."

The public were unsympathetic. Arrow had a reputation for being obsessed with efficiency, firing anyone who fell behind. His pocket watch was a famous symbol of his cruel fastidiousness.

Six years later, the file revealed something unreported: his famous watch was missing from his body.

Multiple witnesses confirmed Arrow had the watch when he entered the garden. The police thought he'd been attacked and robbed by someone entering via a hole in the chain-link fence.

Arrow's family asked for the case to be represented as an accident, at least until any culprit was caught.

"The answer lies at the bottom of the well, Watson," Holmes said as he prepared to abseil down it.

Minutes later, I hauled him back up, covered in dirt but brandishing the watch!

"Perhaps it was an accident," I suggested.

"Always a possibility," said Holmes. "But note the pocket watch is broken from the chain. We cannot eliminate murder yet."

Holmes considered there to be three suspects: Arrow's gardener, Archibald Bloggs, a former criminal; Arrow's wife, Cordelia, his sole inheritor; and Arrow's manservant, Michael Stammers, last to see him alive.

Bloggs now worked for a different estate nearby, and we found him pruning their hedges.

"He was a hard man, true to his reputation," he said. "I was the fifth head gardener he had hired that year, but I kept a very tight ship. Still do."

"No doubt operating a crew of cracksmen in your youth gave you a good work ethic," said Holmes.

"True enough," said Bloggs without shame. "Timing is everything in a robbery. But I paid my debt and Arrow knew my past."

"Would he often walk in the garden?" Holmes asked.

"No, he was barely here. He would usually visit just long enough to dismiss a few members of staff he considered tardy. I was on the other side of the estate on the day he fell in the well. Someone had given him the impression there was a blockage, and he went to investigate. It's a shame; if he'd waited for me, I could have told him there wasn't one. At that point."

At that point, I thought, but chose not to express it.

"If he had intended to fire you that day, you got a rather lucky break, shall we say," said Holmes.

"Two other gardeners were with me when he fell in. When they said he fell in," said Bloggs.

"And I was dismissed anyway. They blamed me for his 'accident.' But the fence wasn't actually my responsibility; it was a security measure that his butler, Stammers, oversaw. I heard them arguing about repairs that morning."

Cordelia Arrow, a very fearful woman, would only meet us in the company of most of her household retinue, including Stammers.

"Phineas was always right; that was his curse," she sniffed. "He felt the world should be a perfect machine. He knew he was infallible: the cleverest, the strongest, the best at climbing and hunting. But every person, every part that wasn't him, was defective!"

She lifted a handkerchief to wipe her eye, then recoiled at a speck of dust on it.

"Eurgh!" she cried. It was removed and replaced with a pristine one.

"The only thing he felt worked correctly was that watch," she continued. "It was Swiss, belonged to his father. He had it in and out of his pocket so often, he went through chain after chain..."

"Did you speak to him that morning, about a supposed blockage in the well?" asked Holmes.

"My goodness, no!" she cried. "I never concern myself with anything to do with that beastly jungle."

"You don't know if he intended to fire Mr. Bloggs?"

"Phineas rarely planned his firings; they were split-second decisions. Why, he's dismissed Stammers dozens of times, only to hire him back a day later. He's the only person who really knows how to run this place."

She nodded toward him, and we adjourned to the servants' quarters with him.

"The master had indeed heard the well had become blocked," Stammers informed us. "I think now that it was one of the younger gardeners' misunderstanding how the well operates. It often fills up when the tide comes in."

"Did you argue with him that morning? About repairs?" said Holmes.

"Yes," said Stammers. "I had so many duties that I fear one or two of them did slip, and he was right to be unhappy. The links had become worn. But I could not repair them until he was in bed."

"What does that have to do with the fence?" I asked. But Holmes simply stood and walked out of the room.

"You've solved it?" I asked.

"A circular puzzle, like a watch face. I simply had to look for the connections... or lack thereof."

Question: Who does Sherlock Holmes think is responsible for Phineas Arrow's death?

27 The Golden Snuffbox

"It was an accident," said Sergeant Ardron. "I didn't know that if you wrote an "A" on a file, then the case... stopped existing. The case in question wasn't mysterious or difficult. It was solved."

Oliver Boardman had a valuable golden snuffbox stolen while having lunch at Von Trapp's Cafe, in Stow-on-the-Wold. He had left it on the table.

"Luckily I was sitting nearby; saw it all!" said Sergeant Ardron. "I stood up and arrested the woman, Miss Jankis, and brought her here to the station. She confessed. I put her statement in the folder, and was going to write 'AA' on it, for Alan Ardron, when I got distracted after the first 'A.' On my return, the file was gone, and I got an anonymous message telling me never to speak of it again. That was three years ago."

"And Miss Jankis?" asked Holmes.

"We had to release her. Sorry if you wasted your time."

"I find it unlikely that Ardron rose to the rank of Sergeant without knowing about the Anathema Archive," said Holmes as we left the station. "He sent this case there for a reason."

First, we visited Oliver Boardman. He was a baker in the town and was surprised to see us.

"We are investigating the theft of the snuffbox," said Holmes.

"You mean three years hence?" Boardman said hesitantly.

"That's right," said Holmes, and Boardman looked strangely relieved. "Was it stolen before or since?" Holmes continued.

"Oh! No. I wasn't certain if you meant my snuffbox," Boardman said. "Yes, it was taken, but the woman had it for mere seconds before Alan... that policeman intervened."

"May we see it?" Holmes asked.

"I'll get it," said Boardman, ducking below the counter.

"You don't keep it with you?" asked Holmes.

"I've quit snuff," Boardman said, emerging with a gaudy, bejewelled golden snuffbox. He looked nervous as Holmes examined it.

"So you have. It's empty," Holmes said, opening it. "Do you often go to Von Trapp's Cafe?"

"Oh, no. Well, occasionally," Boardman said.

As we left, Holmes showed me the tips of his fingers.

"Snuff?" I asked.

"Gold paint," he said.

Von Trapp's Cafe was gaudily decorated, but empty of customers. Henry Von Trapp, the proprietor, was just hanging up the phone.

"Gentlemen! Would you like a table?"

"Yes please, two cups of Earl Grey," said Holmes. I was surprised as I expected him to get to questioning immediately, as was Von Trapp, seemingly.

After the worst cup of tea I had had in years, Holmes spoke to Von Trapp about the incident.

"Ah yes, Mr. Boardman was here and put his snuffbox on the table by accident. The lady, I forget her name, stared at it for some time before suddenly standing up and walking past the table. I did not realize what she had done until Alan stood up and grabbed her hand."

"It must have been bad for your reputation, to have a theft here. Especially when the thief was allowed to go free," said Holmes.

"Yes, I got a letter about that, saying I had to say nothing," said Von Trapp with irritation. "But while that became a secret, people started gossiping about other thefts occurring here, as you probably have heard."

"With the sergeant in here so often, that hardly seems likely," I remarked.

"Oh, he is not a frequent customer at all. I barely know him," said Von Trapp.

The thief, Miss Ada Jankis, reluctantly agreed to speak to us in Hyde Park, London, once we said she wouldn't be arrested.

She was a care-worn, nervous young lady.

"I never done anything like it before, God's oath. But it was right there. And I had so many money troubles," she said, wringing her hands. "I was passing through the town, looking for work."

"You asked for work in the cafe?"

"I did, no luck. The man offered me a free cuppa out of pity."

"Then you took the snuffbox?" said Holmes.

"Yeah. He wasn't looking. And he'd just been boasting to the bloke who ran the cafe about how he didn't need it, didn't even like it much, he said. Nothing to him, everything to me."

"And then Sergeant Ardron grabbed you?" said Holmes.

"Is that his name? It all happened so fast I don't know if I even caught it," she said. "Yeah, he was right next to me almost immediately, shouting 'You're nicked, you filthy thief!' like in a story."

She started crying.

"I cried then, too," she said. "And he said, 'well, maybe.' And I said '... If I turn myself in?' I knew where the police station was, so I immediately put the box down and headed

in that direction. He took me inside, questioned me and then suddenly I was being let go, told it was all over, forget it ever happened. Then I really cried."

"Who let you go? Ardron?" Holmes asked.

"I can honestly say it was too much of a blur," she said.

As we left, Holmes nodded.

"There was an accident," he said thoughtfully. "But without it, there would have been many more crimes, and victims."

Question: Who does Sherlock Holmes suspect Sergeant Ardron was trying to protect?

Hint: Alan.

28 The Impenetrable Fortress

Stone Security Solutions were at the forefront of home protection, and Lord Bernard Stone's fortress of an office building, where we were currently hiding, had all of its most popular products: unscalable spiked walls, blinding lights, and a one-of-a-kind experimental locking mechanism.

One year ago, Lord Stone's office had been broken into, and documents stolen. Lord Stone pressured the police to send the case to the Anathema Archive.

"The burglary would have destroyed our profits," Lord Bernard said. "The thief exploited a flaw in the locking mechanism. This new system is not used anywhere else, but the robbery would cast a pall over our entire range..."

"Have you fixed the flaw?" Holmes asked.

"No," Lord Bernard said. "I thought the criminal would return; I could face him myself. I've slept in my office for a year, and no sign."

"Why would he return? What was stolen?" said Holmes.

"Plans for other experimental security devices," said Lord Bernard. "Incomplete. I thought he would return for the rest."

"Your burglar is aware of your residence," said Holmes. "You must make a big show of leaving; Watson and I will lay in wait instead. We need a copy of the key."

"There's only one key," said Lord Bernard. "It's impossible to copy, which is why the crime is so confounding. But here."

He handed Holmes the door key. And I could see that, bafflingly, it had no notches, ridges or teeth. It was a smooth rectangle.

"Obviously I cannot explain how it works," he said.

I thought Holmes might already know. But if he did, he had not deigned to explain it to me. He did let me inspect the key. I could find not a single mark on its surface.

Holmes returned with an iron rasp in his hand.

"Apologies, Watson, I was pursuing an alternative theory about someone wearing down the iron bars at the rear entrance. But they're remarkably strong," he said, putting the rasp in his pocket and dusting iron filings off his hands.

As we sat and waited, Holmes explained who he considered most likely to step through the door.

"First, Dr. Jakob Harket. Formerly employed by Lord Bernard, not in his locksmith department, but as an electric fence consultant."

"Electric fences? Barbaric!" I exclaimed.

"I concur, though there are some cattle ranchers in the United States who use it. Harket is a volatile man, enthusiastic about the punitive applications of electricity. Lord Bernard insists he was dismissed before development of the new locking system and would have had no knowledge of its operation," said Holmes.

"Could he have calculated how it functions?" I asked.

"Possibly. His expertise lies outside of locksmithing. Our second suspect is Leander Loudermilk, owner of Loudermilk's Locksmiths..."

"I've seen their advertisements," I said.

"Mr. Loudermilk is Lord Bernard's primary competitor and an expert locksmith," said Holmes, passing me a newspaper article. I put the key on the table and read it. Loudermilk was quoted as saying that Lord Bernard's company had successfully shown people how important it was to have solid security for their homes and workplaces, but his prices were so high that they should use Loudermilk Locksmiths instead. He was high on the list of suspects.

I reached for the key but found it had gone. Or so I briefly thought. It was next to a table lamp. Had it moved? Surely my imagination.

"Finally, we have Lord Stone's twin brother, George Stone."

They were identical twins, but as titles passed to the firstborn it was Bernard Stone who became a Lord, due to having been born mere seconds before George. However, several years ago George had produced a nurse who claimed to have been present at the birth and

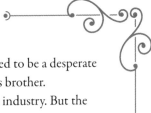

would testify that it was George who was born first. This was later proved to be a desperate scheme, and Lord Stone had understandably distanced himself from his brother.

"George Stone has no technical acumen, or even connections in the industry. But the police suspected him simply because of that."

Holmes pointed at what appeared to be a camera lens implanted above the door frame.

"The investigators thought there might be a camera-based trigger to the lock. As George is identical to Bernard, his face would open doors, as they say," said Holmes.

"Is that true?" I asked.

"Give me the key," said Holmes. I passed it to him, noting with confusion that as he took it, it was suddenly covered in what looked like large specks of dirt.

"Truthfully, Watson, Lord Stone's device depends on a simple scientific principle, and that makes it much less secure than a simple, ordinary key."

Then we heard a kind of whirring, clunking sound behind us at the door. The lights flickered as our culprit stepped through the door.

Question: Who does Sherlock Holmes think has broken into Lord Stone's office?

Hint: Metal.

29 The Flying Needletail

The train thundered along the track at teeth-rattling speed. Outside, the thunderstorm raged in the darkness. The engine room, sealed on all sides and accessible only by a single locked door, was unbreachable. The engineer stood outside it with us, the fireman lay unconscious in the dining car along with seven others. We feared the worst.

No one was in control of The Flying Needletail.

On the wildly winding tracks of the Scottish Highlands, a crash could happen at any moment.

Holmes had read the file about how the train's designer, Festus MacGillicuddy, was arrested for embezzlement. The file contained some cryptic documents that led Holmes to realize MacGillicuddy had passed details about the train's design to persons unknown. Holmes surmised it was connected with the train's inaugural journey from London Paddington to Edinburgh, and arranged to be on board.

There were seven crew members: the engineer, stoker, conductor, brake man, the dining car's waiter, and two guards for the luggage carriage. There were also ten passengers, luminaries from the head executive of the North British Railway Company (owners of the train), to Sarnum Dospa, controversial Maripotanian ambassador.

A large quantity of gold bullion was secretly stowed in the luggage carriage. NBRC wanted to demonstrate that their train was a secure way of transporting valuable items.

We were in the luggage area with Liam McCracken, the primary guard. He had just changed shifts with the other guard, who had gone to the dining car. McCracken had the only key to the cargo, and was enthusiastic to defend against theft.

"Let them try!" he crowed, patting his revolver.

"Have you noticed any unusual actions from the passengers or crew?"

McCracken shrugged. "The engineer, Jacob Hegarty, drinks a lot, but he's a steady hand. That brake man isn't from here, so that's suspicious, but I doubt he has the guts to steal anything. And the passengers are all big wigs; they probably don't need any more gold."

"Actually, Iain Cleeves, the transportation magnate, has extensive underworld connections," said Holmes casually. "He's very comfortable about the idea of stealing and having more gold."

McCracken gritted his teeth. "Well then, tell me if you see him."

Suddenly the train's brake man, Patrick Shaver, ran in.

"The passengers are... passing out. I do not understand."

We rushed to the dining car to find nine passengers, the other security guard, and the train's stoker lying on the floor.

"It may have been the tea," said Shaver, indicating a few smashed cups. "I have also drunk some. But not much."

Holmes sniffed the cup, then looked up sharply.

"Has the engineer drunk the tea?" he asked quickly.

"I don't know," replied Shaver, and Holmes immediately jumped up. We all three hurried through the carriages toward the engine.

"In truth, if the engineer is passed out, it is more likely to be from drink than drugged tea," said Shaver. "He has been belligerent and hateful, and with the stoker unconscious."

"Is it wise to have such a fellow in charge of the train?" I asked.

Shaver shrugged.

"I cannot criticize. There is a man on this train I loathe, but I serve with a smile. Perhaps it is better to be passionate, true to yourself."

The engineer was not passed out. Instead, we found him locked out of his own engine, barely coherent.

"I can't breach this door," said Holmes. "The only access is with the key. I was a fool to concentrate my attentions on the luggage carriage. We are woefully behindhand on this entire scheme."

Jacob Hegarty looked bitterly resigned.

"I was quenching me thirst when someone grabbed me from behind, coshed me. When I came to, 30 minutes had passed. I was out here, and the engine room locked. My key is gone. If, as you say, the stoker's out cold, that means this train's a rampaging bull with nae matador! I warned them this could happen with a lockable engine. I told them to give someone else a key. They never listen. And now we're all dead! DEAD!"

He screamed the last, then slumped to the ground.

"So you had the only key?" said Holmes.

"As a safety precaution," Hegarty mumbled. "The engine's state-of-the-art; they didn't want competitors filching their designs."

Holmes pulled me aside and spoke with incredible speed and precision.

"Assume there is only one key. There are three people who may have it. First, our

dramatic friend here. He locked it himself as an act of self-destruction. Second, Liam McCracken. He is in league with someone who wants the gold. Third, Patrick Shaver, using the crash as a self-sacrificing assassination of the ambassador of Maripotania. His accent is that of its rebellious Northern province. Three people. We must choose."

"I assume you already know," I said.

"It's a simple matter of numbers," he said.

Question: Who does Sherlock Holmes suspect holds the key to the engine room?

Hint: 30 minutes.

30   The Deadly Yardarm

A tontine is where groups of families consolidate their wealth, and then pay an equal stipend to their children.

However, when one of the beneficiaries of a tontine dies, the share the others receive grows. Some tontines even decide that once there is only one surviving recipient, they receive all the money. This makes the arrangement a kind of sport where the goal is not to die, or even eliminate the "competition," although most tontines had clauses against (proven) murder.

In 1854, twelve rich families formed a tontine called "The Oak Leaf Arrangement," their twelve sons the beneficiaries. By 1890 only three sons remained due to various diseases and misadventures, although no suspected murders. These men, now in their fifties, became that strange mix of close friend and bitter rival that the upper classes excel at cultivating. Crispin Haversham, Nigel Walston, and Alexander Todhunter decided that rather than try to carefully guard their health and safety and subsist on the already generous payments that the tontine provided, they would instead challenge each other to ever more risky activities and ventures. From tiger hunting in India to mountain climbing in Nepal, they tried it all, egged on by their families, who apparently treated it almost like a spectator sport.

So, when they all embarked on a yacht together to try to win the Harpooner's Cup, nobody was surprised. When they failed to turn up at the designated rendezvous point for the first leg, their families were somewhat concerned, and then horrified when their yacht was found floating adrift with their three dead bodies on board.

"The grim assessment that the family then undertook..." said Holmes, examining the inquest documents, "...was to ascertain which of the men was the last to die."

"Because that man's family would get the money?" I asked.

"Yes. Imagine their outrage when a frustrated magistrate decided to stamp the whole thing with an A, leaving them in a form of legal limbo with no recourse," said Holmes.

"Is the Anathema Archive truly that powerful?" I said with wonder. "It can silence three wealthy families?"

"I am still getting the measure of the Archive's reach and resources. But yes, it can," said Holmes. "And only now can I try to shine light on this incident."

The witness reports from the yacht's discovery said that all three men were found lying on the deck of the boat. The deck was wet, but the undersides of the bodies were dry, and this combined with a few other factors suggested to investigators that they had not moved from the position in which they had fallen.

"Passable deductive work. In fact, before the case was sent to the Archive, each of the families hired private investigators to make their case. A shameful waste of resources," said Holmes.

Each of the men had a wound at the back of their heads, enough trauma to cause unconsciousness and death. One of them, Crispin, had a wound on the front of his head as well. This, combined with the position of the broken yardarm, led all investigators to reach the conclusion that the yardarm had swung round and hit all three of them, knocking them to the deck where they all suffered fatal head injuries.

"They found a partially empty champagne bottle, and three wine glasses, two broken," said Holmes. "So, they may have been too intoxicated to see it coming. Supposedly their bodies were too waterlogged to be successfully subjected to toxicology tests."

The Haversham family's investigators argued that Crispin was last to die. His body was furthest from the middle of the yacht. The yardarm would have swung round in a circular arc, so he would be last to be hit. The other investigators suggested that Crispin's inferior health, combined with lack of sailing experience, meant he would have died sooner.

"The Walstons' investigators argued that Nigel, who stood between Crispin and Alexander, had the smallest wound on the back of his head, and combined with his strong constitution, would have lasted longer. The other investigators said Nigel Walston could not handle alcohol as well as the others.

"The Todhunters said Alexander survived the longest because, despite being closest to the yardarm and most likely to have been hit first, he seemed to have carved the letters POI into the deck, which would have taken time.

"They claimed he was carving the name of his fiancée, Polly," said Holmes. "The other investigators disputed this, as the only knife on board was found in Crispin Haversham's pocket. But on examining the photograph, I'm sure it was Todhunter who carved it."

"It seems impossible to determine who died last," I said.

"Watson, you, like the investigators, are missing a key element here. If they all died the same way, why is there a discrepancy in their wounds? The yardarm was not the only instrument of death on board... "

Question: Who does Sherlock Holmes think died last on board the yacht?

Hint: Forehead wound.

31 The Sinister Stairs

A man disappeared at a boarding house in Nuneaton, 18 months ago. The house's two residents were Bob Smith, a night watchman who occupied the ground floor, and Fulton Sirk, a fishmonger on the second. The first floor's rooms had been sealed up by the landlady, Mrs. Gertrude Creedy.

Algy Williamson, a local thief, bore a grudge against Sirk after a previous altercation. Sirk had awoke one morning to find Williamson going through his possessions, having picked the door lock. Sirk jumped up and Williamson bolted out of the room.

"He made for the stairs, but I had my trousers off! I look out the front window to see if there's anyone what can grab him, and Bob's coming back from night shift. I shout 'Bob, Williamson's coming down the left stairs, grab him!' Bob then charges in the front door. I've got me trousers on, so I run down the left stairs. I get to the first floor landing and Bob's already there, confused. I asked where Williamson is, he turns round and says he don't know!"

"He entered the first floor flat? Climbed through a window?" I suggested.

"The flat is bricked up. And there's no windows on that landing. We ran down and there was no sign of him. Vanished."

"You threatened him; surely you'd be happy to see him vanish," said Holmes.

"I ain't a murderer," said Sirk.

At the boarding house Holmes inspected the stairs, then had the landlady open up the flat on the first floor.

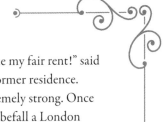

"I think they made this story up so they could get out of paying me my fair rent!" said Mrs. Creedy as we watched a workman unbrick the entrance to her former residence.

As the bricks were removed, the stench of decay and rats was extremely strong. Once we saw inside, we saw every unpleasant creature or malady that could befall a London residence.

"It's been sealed up; what did you reckon would happen?" Mrs. Creedy said sourly. "I was protecting them."

"This damage has existed for years," Holmes observed. "You only sealed it last November."

Holmes could see that the brick wall was solidly built, and there was no evidence of any other access, as well as no evidence that Algy Williamson had ever been inside.

"Did you know Mr. Williamson?" Holmes asked Mrs. Creedy.

"No, I'm a respectable lady," she said indignantly. "Never spoken to the wretch. Bad enough I have to rent houses to these people; I don't mix with guttersnipes." Sirk's rooms were small but well kept. A few tiny windows, none that anyone larger than a cat could crawl through, even if Williamson had somehow remained there.

Smith's rooms had the tiny windows taped up with black paper to prevent light filtering in. When we entered, it was pitch dark. It was so quiet I instinctively drew my gun.

"Lamp's on the left of the door," Smith's voice mumbled as he pulled himself up in bed.

Embarrassed at my alarm, I put my gun away so I could turn the lamp switch and illuminate Bob Smith's messy rooms. He was fairly bleary, as we were talking to him during the day, but I got the sense that even at his sharpest he was a fairly blunt tool.

"It was all a blur!" he said. "I'm just coming back from work when Fulton leans out of the top window and shouts, 'Williamson's coming down the left stairs, stop him!' I don't hesitate; Fulton's a bostin' fellow, so I charge in and run up the stairs. By the time I gets to the first floor I think hang on a tick, where is he? Suddenly I hear someone behind me, so I spin round but it's Fulton. I says to him if I come up the left stairs and you come down the left stairs, where's Williamson?"

"Do you have any reason to suspect Mr. Sirk of lying?"

"No! He's very honest. And it didn't matter because I saw Williamson in the little windows coming down the stairs above the first floor! I even heard his tromping footsteps! But then they just faded. I tell you it's frightened me for weeks; I can barely sleep through the day. I never use them stairs anymore if I'm visiting Fulton."

We left the house and Holmes, his brow knitted, suddenly smacked his forehead!

"Watson, I have been... no, not an idiot. The opposite. Too clever. I had to adjust my sights," he said.

"I'm the wrong person to ask; you know I shoot with my right hand even though I mostly use the left."

"That's exactly the point," said Holmes.

Question: Who does Sherlock Holmes suspect is responsible for Algy Williamson's disappearance at the boarding house?

Hint: Misunderstanding

32 The Willing Prisoner

The supposed reforms of Newgate Prison secured by Elizabeth Fry 50 years ago had not endured. I thought no sane person would willingly choose to be thrown into this gaol.

One year ago, Sir Joseph King was burgled by two unknown men. A few months later, three culprits were found selling the goods. Two of them had no chance to escape. But one of them, hiding in the back room, willingly came out and surrendered.

"We had no idea three men were involved. He said he was the planner, wasn't even on the scene," said Sergeant Medway. "If he hadn't walked out, we would never have even known about him."

"He has another reason to be in prison," said Holmes. "Which man was it?"

"Well. They're triplets. The Book brothers," said Medway sheepishly. "I couldn't remember which of them was in the back room."

"So, you sent the file to the Archive?" I asked.

"I never thought I'd have to talk to you," he said.

Benson, Brian, and Bolivar Book, three notorious criminals with specialities. We spoke to Benson, the digging and demolition expert, while he was sewing mail bags.

"You think I wanna be in here?" he said as he shook some dirt out of one of the bags. "I'd even rather be breaking rocks in the yard. I'd given up the life. Navvy work is hard but less dangerous. I've dug half the London underground. Then those two lackwits turn up, 'easy money, blah blah.' Took the job just to shut them up."

"Would they want to be here?" asked Holmes.

Benson shrugged. "Bolivar wants to be a crime lord; maybe he reckons he'll make connections? This ain't the Reform Club."

"There are a few former members here, though," said Holmes. "Harold Grout over there, for example. Rather surprised to end up here."

Benson looked at a portly gentlemen doing poor stitching on a bag.

"And Brian," he said, "He only cares about money. None of that in here."

Brian Book, the planner, was in his cell reading.

"Yeah, yeah, a Book with a book," he said before we could comment. "I've heard it a million times."

"Mysterious treasures of London," said Holmes, reading its cover. "Fiction?"

"Yeah," Brian said cagily. "Can I help you?"

When Holmes suggested any of the brothers might wish to be in Newgate, Brian nodded.

"Bolivar. A man should never be the nose for his own brother, but if he keeps on thinking this place is a doorway to success, he needs to wake up. That's why he lied about us doing the job that got us in here."

"You claim to be innocent? But you all confessed," I said.

"None of us ever set foot in that house. But when we realized Bolivar had plans to be in here, we copped to it. You'll get us out, won't you, Mr. Holmes?" said Brian, his voice quivering.

Bolivar, the most charming of the brothers, was eating a small bowl of gruel in the refectory. He chuckled weakly when we told him of his brothers' comments.

"Hogwash," he said. "They're pulling your legs. I didn't even realize I was being pulled into a crime when I was there that day; I thought they were simply showing me the plans of his house. Brian has been obsessed with 'hidden treasure' for years; he thinks the world is a pirate island. But he's got weak arms so he can't dig."

"He said he was worried about your safety in here," said Holmes.

"He should worry about Benton," said Bolivar. "He's always getting dragged off to that Grout man's cell. He's made himself a little fiefdom here and Benton keeps crossing him. I dread to think the beatings he has received."

Holmes and I went to see the governor of the prison, Ferdinand Cress, to ask about the brothers' conduct.

"They're all model prisoners," he said blankly. "Do the work, don't make trouble. We're running a pretty tight ship here."

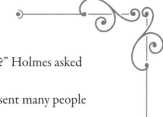

"You're not concerned about any illicit activities or mistreatment?" Holmes asked coldly.

"If you've seen any, please report it, Mr. Holmes. After all, you've sent many people here," the governor said with a shrug.

Holmes was in a black mood as we left. "I try to serve the law as best I can. But when the ultimate destination is that place, well, it tends to blunt my enthusiasm for this pursuit."

"But which brother willingly got himself sent there?" I asked him.

"Oh, yes. Well, let's just say I could have a word with the governor, and that the prison would have at least one less occupant. But one of those events might actually preclude the other…"

Question: Who does Sherlock Holmes suspect willingly entered Newgate Prison?

Hint: Dirt.

33 The Uncursed Necklace

Seven years ago, Peter Garton left his house and went to a goldsmith where he purchased a diamond necklace for his sister, Katie. After he had left the store, he was never seen again. No body was found, and the case was sent to the archive by a superstitious policeman who heard that the necklace was cursed.

We visited Garton's wife, Henrietta, in the townhouse where she lived with his two sons.

"If I'm honest, I barely saw him while we were married. He had his business, his clubs, I don't know what else, but it kept him busy. His sister saw more of him that me," she said.

"You have no idea where he went?" said Holmes.

"I was in the front room when he left; he said he was going to buy his sister a birthday present. That was the last I saw him. I imagine after he visited the goldsmith he may have gone to his club."

"No other possibilities?" asked Holmes.

"Our maids at the time were useless, so I kept finding betting slips for the dog track carelessly strewn around our house. Perhaps he went there. I'm not telling you anything that I didn't tell the police at the time."

"Might he have met friends there who could account for his presence?" asked Holmes.

"Once again, you are asking the wrong person," Mrs. Garton said coldly. "But I would say that he had few actual friends. He went to his club to smoke and drink, and to the dog track to gamble."

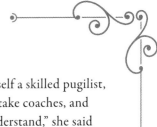

"So, what do you believe happened?" asked Holmes.

She pursed her lips. "Peter had very little fear. He thought himself a skilled pugilist, a brilliant marksman. He preferred to walk the streets rather than take coaches, and would often visit the grimier parts of the city, I was brought to understand," she said with distaste.

The goldsmith who had sold Peter Garton the necklace, Leonard Baxter, still operated his shop in Hatton Garden. He was a bluff, jolly fellow who seemed more like a big-game hunter than a goldsmith.

"Oh yes, Pete was almost like a brother to me," he said. "Miss him every day. Met him at the club a decade ago; there were a lot of puffed-up popinjays there, but I could see he had real strength at his core. I tried to give him a preferential rate on the necklace, but he insisted on paying full price."

"Did he say where he was going afterward?" asked Holmes.

"He told me he was heading to the dog track in Hendon, then to his sister's house, 34 Finchley Road," Baxter said. "He asked me if I wanted to come along, but I had another important client coming that day. It's a shame, because the client rearranged anyway and I missed out on the chance. Not to go to the dog track, I don't particularly care for gambling, but I could have strolled with him dipping into the tobacconists, the tailor, and the milliners on Brent Street."

He looked regretful.

"What do you believe happened to him?" asked Holmes.

"He felt very confined by life here in the city," Baxter said. "I wouldn't be surprised if he's off in some jungle somewhere having the time of his life."

His sister somehow seemed more contemptuous of him than his wife did.

"My brother had no interest in anything other than his own enjoyment," she said, tutting. "He would often try to ply me with gifts, but it was usually because our parents had caught a whiff of his transgressions and he wanted me to help him pull the wool back over their eyes. I regret to say I gave in too many times."

"Were you expecting him that day?" asked Holmes.

"Yes, he had sent me a message asking me to be in for 'a nice surprise.' I saw through it immediately. I don't regret never getting the necklace. I don't believe in curses, but it sounds like a real eyesore."

"What do you think happened to him after he left the shop?" asked Holmes.

"Oh, I imagine he wandered off to some back alley to watch men punching each other, or animals tearing each other apart. Then someone saw the ridiculous necklace and decided to help themselves. He was always boasting about the encounters he had with 'ruffians,' people confronting him, or following him around in the shadows. Never any tales of comradeship or camaraderie," she said, tutting.

As we left, Holmes found the nearest policeman and instructed him to rush as quickly as he could to headquarters.

"You know who is responsible for his death?" I asked.

"I'm certain I do. Because they were certain as well," said Holmes.

Question: Who does Sherlock Holmes suspect murdered Peter Garton?

Hint: Details.

34 The Misplaced Cadaver

"Five months ago, the archaeologists on a Bronze Age burial site in Lincolnshire were exhuming corpses when they discovered one in modern clothing," said Holmes to me in the coach. "The investigator thought the death was supernatural and sent it directly to the Archive."

Our first stop was the morgue.

"Male, middle-aged, advanced decay," Holmes said. "Expensive clothing, 20 years out of fashion. Flecks of varnished wood. Mud renders further forensic analysis difficult."

The excavation was in a vacant lot close to the village. The frozen muddy ground had deep wheel ruts. A cart hit one of the ruts, jolting a crate onto the ground.

"I said to secure them!" shouted a woman with an Italian accent. "Idiota!"

This was Alessandra Divola.

"The so-called archaeologists here cannot believe a woman or foreigner can do their job," she said fiercely.

"You found the body?" asked Holmes.

"Yes. I did not recognize it, or the clothes."

"You had a disagreement with a Mr. Gerald..."

"More murder accusations!" she interrupted. "Simkins stole the credit of others. He disappears and suddenly I'm the viper who stole British archaeology's shining light!"

"You stabbed him? Twice?" asked Holmes.

"With a hat pin! I am sure you know why," she said.

"How did the others react to the corpse?" Holmes asked.

"Shock. Turvey acted suspiciously, as usual. Idiotic thug. Simeon Belgeddes was there, which was strange."

"Why?"

"He normally works at night. He was there in that floppy hat and dark glasses looking surprised," she said with a frown.

I concurred with Miss Divola's assessment of Roger Turvey. He seemed more like a confidence trickster than an archaeologist.

"I own this land," he said. "So, it was serendipitous I found this site."

"Mr. Turvey told you there might be Saxon remains here?" asked Holmes. "There's no record of you as an archaeologist before the dig began. You have a former conviction for fraud."

"Cannot a man repent and find a new vocation?" asked Mr. Turvey. "Mr. Scarley, the head undertaker, took a chance in hiring me ten years hence. It was my work with bodies that led me to archaeology."

Mr. Turvey pointed at the building next door where a sign read: Scarley & Turvey, General Undertakers.

"When the body was found, did you think it might have been from your undertakers?" asked Holmes.

"We would never misplace the deceased! I think it's some vagrant who drunkenly stumbled into the area."

"So, you don't think it is Gerald Simkins?" asked Holmes.

"I did, briefly. I wouldn't be surprised if he had come a cropper, especially with that Italian woman about. But he wrote me a letter from Europe. Somewhere out of the way where communication is difficult," Turvey said quickly.

As darkness fell, Simeon Belgeddes arrived at the site. The growing moonlight made his face look almost bone white, with cheekbones even more pronounced than Holmes' and a mysterious smile.

"Of course, I was mortified when I saw the body, if you'll pardon the pun," he intoned. "My first thought was that it was Simkins."

"Does the body resemble him?" asked Holmes.

"Somewhat. The clothes are a little more old-fashioned. And the body seemed like it had died quite a while ago, drained of life, as it were," he said, licking his lips.

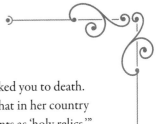

"Did you suspect Miss Divola?" asked Holmes.

"Not really. She jabbed Simkins but she's not a killer. Unless she talked you to death. She's always complaining about English archaeologists; I pointed out that in her country they've barely advanced beyond passing off the hands and feet of peasants as 'holy relics.'"

"You were the one who found this site?" asked Holmes.

"Indeed. I had cause to visit the undertakers and purchase a coffin. I noticed what appeared to me to be a shard of pottery in the adjoining field and informed Mr. Turvey of this, and in pretty swift order he had arranged for a team to begin digging it up. If he had hoped we would find some golden hoard he could sell, he was quite deluded. But he and Mr. Simkins seemed to get along well."

"Why did you need a coffin?" asked Holmes.

"For a friend. They have a roaring trade in them next door, carting them in and out and sending them off to all parts of England, even other countries, I've heard. No idea why any true Englishman would want to be buried abroad," said Belgeddes, shuddering. "If you're interested in my thoughts, I have a book coming out this year."

But Holmes was already walking away from him and peering at the ruts at the entrance.

"Of course," he said. "A ridiculous scheme, certainly, but no more ridiculous than the idea of vampires."

Question: Who does Sherlock Holmes suspect is responsible for the appearance of the body in the dig?

Hint: Decay.

35 The Perplexing Puzzle

The will of Timothy McBenzie, the puzzle-loving Laird of Auchtermuchty, revealed he had hidden a great treasure in his conundrum-filled mansion: a goblet covered in jewels. Its location would be revealed only when the sun was about to set. Potential treasure hunters were stalled by his niece's decision to deny access to the mansion.

Then the house's architect, Cyril Ellis, was found dead, apparently poisoned. When the goblet was sold to an American collector, it seemed as if someone had killed the architect to get the truth from him. Three people came forward, each claiming they had solved the mystery, but when they opened the secret panel, it was empty.

McBenzie's niece Elspeth Dunwiddy allowed us to enter the house, deactivating most of its puzzle-based traps and locks. We found ourselves at the top of the main staircase at 6:25 pm.

Light shone through a stained-glass window, projecting a fleur-de-lis on a wooden panel in the wall. Holmes opened the secret panel and confirmed its emptiness.

With us were Mrs. Dunwiddy, McBenzie's friend Hamish Roper, and "treasure hunter" Donald Unstible.

"I hate puzzles," said Mrs. Dunwiddy. "He spent all of his time on them. Then the will turned my ancestral home into a mummy's tomb."

"Yet you discovered the mystery?" asked Holmes.

"I may hate puzzles, but I can solve them. The time of day indicated light was a factor. I wasted two hours passing through the hedge maze looking for a sundial, then found the window and the empty panel."

"Two hours? Surely you know the maze's layout?" said Holmes.

"Irrelevant. Two hours is the minimum amount of time it takes to circumvent, due to its design," she said.

"Who do you think stole the cup?" asked Holmes.

"Roper is an untrustworthy swine. And Unstible's nothing but a grave-robber. I should never have allowed him access."

"You let him into the mansion?" asked Holmes.

"Only the grounds. I thought my father's locks would thwart him. He told me they had; said he'd never entered. But at least he asked, unlike Roper, who broke in. I did wonder why I saw him at the station that afternoon, but I had to run to catch the 4 o'clock train."

"What a privilege!" Hamish Roper said, shaking Holmes' hand.

"You had a dispute with Mrs. Dunwiddy," said Holmes.

"She went against Tim's wishes," Mr. Roper said. "He wanted me to search for the treasure. When I entered the grounds through the maze that afternoon, it was not 'breaking and entering.' I solved the puzzle lock on the back door, and as it is a different combination each time, that is an act of mental effort, not burglary. Also physical effort, as my fingers were numb from the winter cold."

"And you solved the mystery?" asked Holmes.

"Once I saw the light shining through the window, I understood. I opened the panel to find it empty, then she discovered me, shouted about theft. I had to make a quick exit."

Donald Unstible looked like every cliché of a hunter, but seemed more fragile.

"Mrs. Dunwiddy permitted me to enter the grounds on the morning of the 12th of December. I didn't mind I wasn't granted access to the house. I assumed the treasure was in the gardens or the maze."

"You lied to her and told her that you never entered?" said Holmes.

"I sensed she was setting me up. I had every intention of telling her I knew how to open the front or rear puzzle locks. But when I found the treasure vault empty, I suspected she had already taken it for herself, and intended to claim I had stolen the treasure. Hence why she let me in after weeks of requests."

"When the architect was found dead, you came forward?" asked Holmes.

"It seemed the correct thing to do," he said simply.

"How many 'treasures' have you discovered in your career?" asked Holmes.

Mr. Unstible shrugged. "I am at the beginning of this undertaking. It's not a dignified start. Do you know the secret of McBenzie's puzzle locks? Anyone can solve them. They simply delay for 51 minutes and then spring open. He cared more about people feeling clever than he did testing their intellect."

Holmes returned to the window and stared through it at the darkness that lay outside.

"True. And one of you cared so little for puzzles that they would rather kill a man to learn the secret than try and solve the puzzle. The murderer must be the only person who could not have... seen the light."

Question: Who does Sherlock Holmes suspect killed the architect and stole the cup?

Hint: Time.

36 The Five Cherubs

Three years ago, over five consecutive days, five different London restaurants found that someone had thrown a small plaster cherub through their front windows in the night. Monday: Gardner's at 12 Regent Street. Tuesday: The Manticore at 101 Strand. Wednesday: The Vere at 8 Vere Street. Cafe Marseille at 89 Maiden Lane had its window smashed on Thursday, and on Friday it was Smithson's at 34 Paternoster Row.

Only whatever was closest to the window was stolen, except for Smithson's, where 200 pounds was stolen from a safe.

"There were no clues as to the culprit. It may have been one person, or a string of copycats," said Holmes. "It was sent to the Archive by a frustrated police inspector. He didn't consider that the papers had featured stories about every single crime."

The owner of Smithson's was Pierce Smithson. He had closed after the robbery, reopening in a different location.

"Shame, I'd been there since 1893. But I secured investment," he said.

"You said that the safe was opened. Who had the combination?" asked Holmes.

"Only me. I set the combination myself. Eight digits, impossible to guess. I may have written it down once; I think I disposed of the note."

"What was the combination?" asked Holmes.

"I prefer not to say," said Smithson, glancing at a different safe in the corner of his office.

"You have used the same combination for that safe?" said Holmes.

Smithson blushed. "It's difficult to memorize numbers. This new office is much more secure."

Holmes shook his head. "Mr. Smithson your relationship with other restaurant owners is known to be combative."

"It's a cut-throat business. I had no personal animus against the other four restaurants

that had this cherub thrown through their window."

"True. But if your intention was to fake a robbery, for whatever reason, creating a series of false crimes would be an excellent cover," said Holmes, "…even if none of the others had anything stolen from a safe."

"As far as you know," said Smithson. "Shouldn't you find the statues' manufacturer?"

We had. As we entered Athens Wilson's factory, we saw boxes filled with plaster busts of the Queen.

"Once people heard my cherubs had been used to smash windows, most didn't want to buy them, and them that did were up to no good," said Wilson. "I don't associate with that sort anymore."

"You do have a past riddled with criminal associations," said Holmes. "Burglary, robbery with menaces."

"I've reformed, Mr. Holmes," said Wilson. "That's why I made the cherub, a symbol of my rebirth. Someone twisted that with their crimes."

"Who do you suspect?" asked Holmes.

"No idea. My products were on sale to all. If the culprit bought them, it was without

my knowledge. I can't even be seen in the same place as criminals, or my sponsors will withdraw their money. I move in different circles now. I even ate at Smithson's once, and that's not cheap!"

The third suspect was Charlie Lime. He was known as Choking Charlie in the London underworld, due to his habit of visiting restaurants, ordering mutton or some other tough meat, and then pretending to choke, in the hope that the owners would either give him money to pay imaginary medical bills or go away, or another diner would step in to help and be drawn into Charlie's web of deceit.

He had been banned from the five restaurants that had been targeted. But then, it was more difficult to find a restaurant in London that he hadn't been banned from. And furthermore, he actually had what seemed to be a solid alibi.

"I was living in Liverpool at the time of the crimes, Mr. Holmes," Charlie said snidely, sipping a beer in a public house where the only thing that would choke you is the landlord. "On the days in question, I was seen by multiple witnesses in various, ah, establishments. Now, I could have made the journey repeatedly back and forth on the train just to chuck some stone angels through some windows, but that doesn't sound like a good use of time or money, does it?"

"Perhaps you had an accomplice do it," I suggested.

"I am an honest man, Dr. Watson. But if I were to attempt any kind of larceny, I wouldn't have an 'accomplice,'" Charlie said. "Too many people nowadays trust or rely on the help of others. No self-sufficiency. Perhaps I ought to become a lecturer! Or write a series of educational pamphlets. What would you say is the best way to get that information across, Mr. Holmes?"

"It would be worth the journey by train for 200 pounds profit," Holmes suggested.

"Is that how much was in the safe? They never said in the newspapers," said Charlie. "Maybe a newspaperman did it; they certainly made enough money from the crimes, reporting them every day..."

As we left, Holmes' mind was working furiously.

"Of course," he said. "Information. That's the key."

Question: Who does Sherlock Holmes suspect threw the plaster angels through the restaurant windows?

Hint: Numbers.

37 The Angel's Share

Two gentlemen celebrating a business deal uncorked a rare vintage of Irish whiskey that came from Flanagan's famous distillery, on the island of Chorran. They found an '8' burned into the underside of the cork.

"They thought it might be a cry for help from some poor worker," said Holmes. "And so, we must go and find Mary Flanagan."

He explained it all as we took the long journey across England, Wales, and Ireland to get to the small island off the west coast. Mary was the daughter of Liam Flanagan, the distillery's owner. Three months ago, he had reported her missing.

"However, the '8' matches her handwriting," said Holmes.

We were greeted at the dock by Liam Flanagan himself.

"These are not the circumstances in which I would want to welcome you to Chorran," he said. "I wish I were giving you a tour. We have the biggest octagonal still in the country, for example."

"You said you thought your daughter had run away from the island?" said Holmes.

Flanagan nodded solemnly. "Little Mary thought she had grown tired of life here. I blame her nursemaid; she gave her too free a hand, let her run around the island like Robinson Crusoe. I should have paid more attention, but the distillery takes a lot of time, and after her mother passed I didn't have the heart to discipline her."

"Why do you suppose someone wrote an '8' on the underside of a cork in your factory?" asked Holmes.

"No idea. A joke?" said Flanagan.

Holmes asked Mr. Flanagan about possible enemies.

"Fionna Macken," he said. "Her family provided us with water for decades, from a stream in the hills, until she got greedy. We found another stream in the legendary

'bottomless well'! Not so bottomless it seems. And Ciaran Kelly's been fuming for months. He grows the barley for the whiskey but he's worried I'll have to import some since his crop failed."

We hiked several hours to Fionna Macken's cottage.

"Another mountain stream in the 'bottomless well.' Lies!" she exclaimed. "The well's artificial. He keeps his private reserve down there because it's so cold. He tapped my family stream, is what he did."

"You're not boycotting the consumption of his whiskey, though," said Holmes, taking note of a few bottles around her house.

"Well, it's made from my water!" she replied.

"I noticed eight beehives in your garden," said Holmes, always a keen apiarist.

"Well, I've got to do something else to make money," she said. "Hate the wretched things. His daughter loved to come here and play, before she ran off to avoid marrying that Fricker boy."

"Who?" asked Holmes.

"Ah, of course he didn't tell you. Flanagan had her lined up to tie the knot with Michael Fricker's son Patrick, to cement an alliance between two whiskey dynasties. You don't need to know maths to understand one plus one equals seemingly infinite profits for them both!"

Ciaran Kelly seemed a rough-hewn but good-natured man, working in the field as we spoke to him.

"I had nine fields but we've had to abandon one. Subsidence," he said. "I know Mr. Flanagan says he'll keep using only my family's barley, but he's been looking for an excuse to cut us loose for a long time, and if Mary marries Patrick Fricker he'll share his supplier anyway."

"Is that why you think she ran away?" asked Holmes.

"Who said she ran away?" said Kelly. "Sure, it seems like a little island, but there's plenty of places here a person can hide... or be hidden."

"A bottle was opened and it seems she wrote '8' on the cork inside," said Holmes.

"Where might she be to be able to do that?"

Kelly shrugged. "Well the bottling plant's the obvious answer, but she'd be spotted. Truthfully there's bottles of the stuff all over this island. Never let it be said we don't test the stuff before sending it out. Of course, how you'd get it on the boat is the other question."

"I suppose those are filled with grain?" asked Holmes, pointing at the four grain silos arranged in a square next to the farm buildings.

"Not as much as they should be. Mary used to visit here, run around them. Help me with my accounts too, great head for numbers."

After that Holmes and I sat on a nearby stile.

"We've been looking at this whole thing sideways," said Holmes. "Once I realized that, I saw the possibility was... endless."

Question: Who does Sherlock Holmes suspect is keeping Mary Flanagan captive, and where?

Hint: Sideways.

38 The Suspect Usurers

Oleander Gutterbridge was the world's only "resulting detective."

"Because I get results!" he said. Holmes wanted nothing to do with him, yet we would have to visit his offices at 44b Butcher Avenue.

I say his offices, but they were really Holmes'. As I entered, it was uncanny: the slipper full of pipe tobacco, the kerosene desk lamp, the blotter stained with both ink and other chemicals. Blinds in disarray, an antique globe with scratches from thrown knives. A leather chair with the stuffing slightly coming out of one side. In the midst of it all sat Gutterbridge grinning like a loon.

"Mr. Holmes! You seek the assistance of my powers of reduction."

"Deduction," said Holmes through gritted teeth.

"No, I reduce the facts of the case to a sort of informational broth," said Gutterbridge.

When Holmes was "dead," someone in Scotland Yard solicited Gutterbridge's help with a case. The victim was a debt-ridden fruit and vegetable salesman named Bernard Green, violently robbed leaving a pub in Stepney. The suspects were three moneylenders to which he owed money. Gutterbridge questioned each of them at his office, then declared the salesman's injuries were caused by "an avalanche of cauliflowers." The policeman sent it to the Archive to protect his reputation.

"Remember your axiom, Mr. Holmes: once you have eliminated your first idea, your second idea, however ridiculous, must be the truth," said Gutterbridge.

Rather than correct that error, Holmes got Gutterbridge to relate his interrogations. Despite his other deficiencies, he was a diligent transcriber.

"Caractacus White said that he could not have attacked Mr. Green as he was engaged in a fight with another man on the other side of the city, in Battersea. I thought it a bold gambit to avoid prosecution for one crime by admitting another, but then I had not yet

begun to see the extent of his game," said Gutterbridge, trying to pack a pipe while holding a magnifying glass in the same hand.

"Which was?" said Holmes.

"The fight in question was a bare-knuckle boxing match against Bill 'Two-Finger' Sutton. So called because apparently he lacks three fingers on his left hand. Something didn't add up."

"Because White didn't look like a fighter?" I asked.

"No, why would he be called Two-Finger when he has three fingers missing? Surely he should be One-Finger, unless you're counting the thumb. And he has four perfectly good fingers on his right hand; he should at least be Five-Finger..." said Gutterbridge with accompanying hand movements.

"Did anyone corroborate his alibi?" interrupted Holmes.

"I spoke to various crowd members, but for obvious reasons they wouldn't admit to being present. They couldn't even explain about the fingers!"

The second suspect, Philip Took, put on more respectable airs.

"He came in dressed as if visiting the Queen! 'Ah, now the game is on the other foot,' I thought. His alibi was that he was doing charitable works, distributing food amongst the needy. 'At 10 pm at night,' I asked? He preferred to work in the dark, he said. That way people wouldn't know who their benefactor was. This would have the unfortunate side effect of leaving him with no witnesses to his generosity."

"With whom did he claim to be distributing food?" asked Holmes.

"Ah ha!" cried Gutterbridge, pushing a cello off his desk and lifting up a leaflet. "This group, St. Hedwig's society of clandestine givers. They refused to confirm or deny his alibi due to their principles. But I thought it entirely likely that Mr. Took might do this as a way of assuaging his guilt."

"Or it's a front for a criminal organization," replied Holmes, who knew it was.

The final suspect was Rex Heard, late to the appointment.

"He seemed harried, glancing around my office with a look of concern. Although

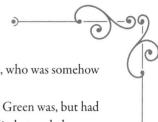

after I heard his explanation, I could understand it," said Gutterbridge, who was somehow wearing two deerstalkers at once.

"He told me that he had in fact been headed to the pub where Mr. Green was, but had been waylaid on the way by a rival of his, Bill Piper. He gave him the slip but ended up slipping on a patch of oil, knocking his lights out! When he awoke, he was tied up inside a paper mill; Piper planned to drown him in ink. Luckily there was some turpentine near his foot, so he kicked it at Piper, blinding him, and found a convenient knife to cut his bonds. Knowing Piper would follow him to the ends of the earth, he decided to try and knock the stuffing out of him, but he said it had just made his problems bigger."

"As if viewed through a magnifying glass," said Holmes.

"Yes! Anyway, seeing as none of their alibis could be corroborated, logically that meant that they were all valid," said Gutterbridge, leaning back.

Holmes shook his head in something like despair. But I also saw in his eyes that he knew exactly who the culprit was.

Question: Who does Sherlock Holmes suspect of attacking Bernard Green?

Hint: Objects.

39 The Fatal Flue

Sir Hugh Brown, a famous financier, had a house with ten fireplaces and ten chimneys, all blazing away. One day, he had them all sealed up, never to be lit again.

Sir Hugh developed a mania for cleanliness after a devastating bout of pneumonia. His home would be a germ-free zone.

"He had everything sealed up with steel and rubber," Holmes said. "Each room had its own pressurized door. The entire mansion was scrubbed with bleach. With no living heirs, he could do as he liked. Sacked almost all his servants."

Then Sir Hugh was found stuffed up one of his chimneys, dead. No one knew how he could have got inside. The chimney was too narrow to climb, especially for the ailing, elderly Sir Hugh. He could not have fallen in, because all the chimneys were sealed at the top with steel plating. Investigators found a hole in the flue at the level of the building's attic, but it was too small for anyone to crawl through.

The suspects were Sigmund DeVries, a German inventor who offered to clean Sir Hugh's house with a new super-vacuum, Hob Aldrich, his former chimney sweep, and Tom Finch, his remaining servant.

We visited DeVries at his laboratory.

"I tried to clean his house to his desire, but it was never enough. I said even if you sealed it all and sterilized the inside, the mansion's age meant dust and dirt were endemic. And those chimneys! Decades of soot inside. Impossible!" he declared.

"What vacuum cleaner did you use?" asked Holmes.

"My V-34," DeVries said, passing us a blueprint of an enormous-looking contraption. "Dismantled now. I have moved on to mechanical sweepers instead."

"Sir Hugh neglected to pay you, is that right?" asked Holmes.

"Indeed, he claimed that I would only get the money when I had finished the job.

But it could not be finished. The amount of suction required would have sucked large objects like furniture. Well, it didn't exist. So, I had to simply accept the loss and move on with my business."

Hob Aldrich employed a large team of chimney sweeps who operated out of Hounslow.

"There's been a lot of advances in the field," said Mr. Aldrich. "The days of sending little lads up the flue are long gone. We have bigger and better brushes than ever before!"

"Were you angry to lose Sir Hugh's business?"

"No. It did concern me to lose the money that ten chimneys brought in. After he'd sealed them, he did ask if I could clean them of soot entirely. I could have lied, but I told him it couldn't be done."

"Could someone have pushed his body into the flue? Or unsealed the chimney, dropped it in?" asked Holmes.

"With great difficulty, perhaps," said Mr. Aldrich. "But why? The investigators thought maybe it was my revenge. When they were stumped, they had me take a look at the chimney. All I could find was that hole at attic level, the size of a rat."

Tom Finch had found employment in another household.

"At first, he was a reasonable man. Passionate, driven, yes, but reasonable. After his pneumonia, he changed. His obsession with cleanliness was a form of madness."

"You were the only servant he kept?" asked Holmes.

"I was the only one who would stay!" he declared. "Sir Hugh required that we all wear special 'clean suits' while inside the house, hermetically sealed rubber coveralls. My word, it was hot inside those things. A few refused and left immediately, and most of the others slyly secured jobs elsewhere. But I stuck it out; I suppose I hoped the mania would pass and I could return to normal duties. But until then, I had to do all the day-to-day tasks. At least he was the only person in the house."

"So in a way his death liberated you?" said Holmes.

"Hardly. It is not easy securing a new household position when your previous employer died in such odd circumstances. Especially if you were the last to see him," he said solemnly.

"Do you recall the events of that day?" asked Holmes.

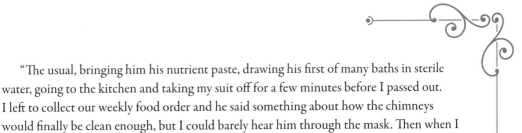

"The usual, bringing him his nutrient paste, drawing his first of many baths in sterile water, going to the kitchen and taking my suit off for a few minutes before I passed out. I left to collect our weekly food order and he said something about how the chimneys would finally be clean enough, but I could barely hear him through the mask. Then when I returned, he was gone, and it was only after days of searching that they found his body."

Holmes considered visiting the house, but ultimately decided it was unnecessary. "I know what happened," he said. "Very improbable, but the truth."

Question: Who does Sherlock Holmes think is responsible for the death of Sir Hugh Brown?

40 The Accusing Effigies

Twenty-five years ago, a golden staff, an heirloom of the Perceval family, was stolen. Centuries before, the family was granted a dukedom and ownership of much of Lincolnshire, provided that every ten years they used the sceptre to perform a ceremony in veneration of the monarch. When the staff was stolen, Duchess Elizabeth Perceval was unable to perform the ceremony and the family lost the title and land.

"I'm certain the thief was one of her children, Alcesta, Noah, or Parker," said Holmes. "But there is a problem: they're all dead. However, in this case, that has not stopped them from talking... in a way."

Perceval Manor, an exceptional example of fifteenth-century architecture, had a crypt filled with many generations of past Percevals.

Thomas Perceval, the son of the previous heir, Noah Perceval, had recently opened the manor to public tours.

"My father and I were denied the dukedom by his brother, Parker Perceval," said Thomas as he led us into the under croft. "When he stole the staff."

He led us to his father's tomb. Noah Perceval had died ten years ago, at 74. The slab held a stone effigy of Noah, rendered in the same dark, stained stone as the crypt. He was dressed as a knight, holding a shield made from a lighter, unstained stone. The shield bore an image of a twisted-looking figure, cradling a staff.

"This detail is an accurate depiction of Parker. My father requested it be included in his effigy to show he believed my uncle stole the staff. Parker knew my father would inherit the dukedom, and I after him. If he couldn't have it, no one could. Ironically, my father never really cared to be Duke. I do."

Parker Perceval died five years before his brother. His tomb had an effigy of him as a knight in the dark, stained stone, with a fierce expression, wielding a sword.

"My uncle was very angry and combative. My father told me he thought Parker wanted to kill him. At first to inherit the dukedom, then later from pure hatred."

He then showed us a detail on the sword, which said in Latin, "Alcesta Rapuit Virga," or "Alcesta stole the staff."

"He loved swords," said Thomas. "I remember weeks before he died, he challenged my father to a sword duel. I was only nine at the time, but I thought it very amusing to imagine this frail 67-year-old man trying to fight my father."

"And he thought your aunt Alcesta had stolen the staff?" asked Holmes.

"Well, clearly not, as he stole it himself. But for some reason he wanted to suggest it. It's ironic, because he was always very genteel with women, especially his mother and sister."

We finally saw the tomb of his aunt, Alcesta, who died only a few months after the staff disappeared.

"She was 73 at the time, so I understand it wasn't a surprise, exactly," he said.

Her dark stone effigy was simpler, showing her wearing a shawl and a peasant's dress. She held a bouquet of flowers, and spelled out on the flowers in plain English were the words, "NOAH TOOK THE STAFF."

"That was a specific request in her will," said Thomas, tight-lipped.

"Why did she believe that?" asked Holmes.

"My father did not like to speak of it," said Thomas. "And as I never met her, I couldn't say. The only thing I could infer is that in the early days when it was missing, she was considered to be the main suspect, as it were, because some of the flowers from the bouquet she was to carry for the ceremony were found near where the staff had once been. That seems to be why Parker accused her, anyway."

Holmes looked thoughtful. "How soon after the staff's theft did your grandmother die?" he asked.

"Roughly two years later. She was 98 years old. To be honest, I think everyone expected her to go at any second; they were surprised that Alcesta predeceased her."

"I see. And these tombs are exactly as their occupants requested?" asked Holmes.

"Yes. Well, obviously, a certain amount of cleaning and maintenance has had to be done. We are admitting visitors, after all, and even without the dukedom the family's reputation must be protected."

"Indeed," said Holmes. Thomas Perceval led us out of the crypt and Holmes took a deep breath of the much fresher air.

"Mr. Perceval was lying," said Holmes. "And that lie is the key to understanding who stole the staff. As is the order in which they died, and the realization that, once they were gone, some, if not all of them, would only seek to tell the truth."

Question: Who does Sherlock Holmes suspect stole the staff?

41 The Rose Rampage

"You took your sweet time!" shouted Rosamond Diddcott as we approached her flower stall in Covent Garden. "Two months ago, I filed that police report!"

There had been a series of attacks on her customers. Each time, they would be knocked down, and a red rose left by their side.

"My roses!" she exclaimed. "Bad enough to deal with the gawping fools who buy my flowers; now people think I'm involved in violence. Sort it out, Holmes."

I sensed why the investigator sent this case to the Archive.

"You deduced my identity. Who do you suspect?" asked Holmes.

"The 'Shropshire Slasher' lives in that building opposite," she said, "my worthless brother wanders around with a stupid rose tattoo on his arm. And plum-pudding-faced Nerys Bumble glares at me from her patch over there."

"The 'Shropshire Slasher?'" said Holmes.

"That's what they call him. Never seen him, but how can they let him live near a decent person like me?"

Miss Bumble's angry expression faltered as we approached her.

"W-what do you want? Sirs?" she stuttered.

"Have you heard about Mrs. Diddcott's customers being attacked?" asked Holmes.

"Oh yes, what a shame. I mean, for them. Not for her. She is a real... ninny," she said uncertainly.

"Have you seen or heard anything strange? Anyone who might bear her a grudge?" asked Holmes.

"Other than me?" Miss Bumble said, shaking a fist theatrically. "Well, she upsets a lot of customers. Which, to be fair, is normal."

She wagged a finger at an old man who was checking a tomato for spots.

"Mr. Figgins, you're an old rascal," she said.

Mr. Figgins looked genuinely upset by this, and Miss Bumble's expression quickly became remorseful.

"Ooh, I'm sorry sir. Have that for free," she stuttered.

"What about Mrs. Diddcott's brother, do you think he may be attacking her customers?" asked Holmes.

"Silly Billy?" she made a dismissive noise. "I've got celery on this stall that has more backbone than that boy."

Fortunately, Billy himself had now appeared and was weaving through the crowds. He had the walk of a triumphant prize fighter, but the physique of one of the more emaciated members of Holmes' Baker Street irregulars.

He puffed up his chest when we began talking to him.

"Billy 'The Rose' Diddcott doesn't attack people on the street," he said.

"Are you not he?" asked Holmes.

"I, uh, that is to say Billy talks about himself in the third personification now," said Billy.

"Well, Mr. The Rose, someone is assaulting citizens and leaving roses at the scene. This may reflect badly upon your intended mythmaking," said Holmes.

"Billy would not leave roses; Billy is the rose," Billy said. "That's my fighting style."

"What exactly is the chosen fighting style of a flower?" I asked.

Billy looked rather confused by this question. "Billy 'The Rose' thinks Miss Bumble might be attacking the people. My, I mean, his, Billy's sister is her competition."

"But they sell different goods. Flowers and vegetables," said Holmes.

"It's all plants! And have you never heard of a cauliflower?" said Billy with the air of a chess player saying "checkmate." We visited the building where Mrs. Diddcott claimed the "Shropshire slasher" lived, and after asking around visited the bedsitting room of a genial, balding man with enormous spectacles, named Isaac Williams.

"It's in the manner of a joke, I believe," he said when asked about his appellation. "I was a knife salesman in Shrewsbury. I don't have a history of violence."

"What about the affray in Kidderminster about three years ago?" said Holmes. "Or was that a different Isaac Williams?"

Mr. Williams' big smile did not entirely vanish, but it lost some of its shine.

"My involvement was misunderstood in that case, Mr. Holmes. I was merely defending myself," he said.

"Are you aware of the recent attacks of the customers of Mrs. Diddcott's flower stall?" asked Holmes.

"Oh my goodness, really?" said Williams. "Are you warning all her other customers that they might be targeted? Because I only bought flowers from her once, I believe. Delightful lady."

He seemed sincere about his latter sentiment, to my surprise.

"No, we just wondered if you may have witnessed anything, due to your vantage point," said Holmes, drawing back Williams' curtain and gazing down at the market, where Mrs. Diddcott was currently having a shouting match with a customer.

"Ah. Sadly not," said Williams. "I did see her brother take an armful of roses from behind her back, but that was a while ago. I hope they can catch the culprit; she certainly suffers enough. She needs someone to protect her, I think."

We left the building and headed back to the stall.

"All very simple," said Holmes. "The oldest story, as the cliché goes."

Question: Who does Sherlock Holmes think has been attacking Mrs. Diddcott's customers?

Hint: Romance.

42 | The Black Cat

Two years ago, on his way to work, fishmonger Harold Gossamer passed the abandoned house in his cul-de-sac and glimpsed a black cat in the window. Unsettled, he kept walking. On his return he saw no cat, but his house's windows were smashed, and cat symbols marked on the walls with soot.

"Next day, I was fired from my job, cut my hand, and was evicted," said Mr. Gossamer.

"You were fired because you didn't bandage your hand and bled on the fish. And your landlord claimed you assaulted him?" asked Holmes.

"I cut my hand, trembling with fear from the curse. Perhaps I did grab my landlord, but he accused me of the vandalism. It was the curse!"

"I thought the house was sealed," said Bolivar Merton, the landlord. "I had to abandon it after a fire. It was structurally sound, but the interior was scorched and ashen. I boarded it up to guard against squatters. After what happened to Mr. Gossamer, I found someone had forced the back door open, even installed their own lock."

"Was anything inside?" asked Holmes.

"A few scraps of meat and some leather collars, but for men, rather than cats," he said. "Too wide in the neck."

"You are also Mr. Gossamer's landlord?" said Holmes.

"Yes. But I only evicted him when he behaved in a hostile manner. He told me he had been fired, and when I asked when he might find employment again, he began shouting about this fiend of a cat and grabbed my lapels. His situation was in no way my fault. Especially as I had to pay for the repair of the broken windows and the cleaning of the house's exterior," he said.

"But you do not own the other two houses in the cul-de-sac?" asked Holmes.

"No, more's the pity. The zookeeper and his wife are relatively innocuous, but it is difficult finding tenants willing to live on the same street as a witch."

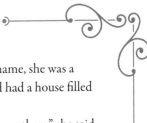

The "witch" in question was Olga Barrington. Despite her Russian name, she was a friendly Mancunian woman who nonetheless did dress in black lace and had a house filled with occult paraphernalia.

"I inherited it all from my aunt. The house, the objects, even Edgar over there," she said, pointing to a large raven perched in the corner of the room. "I assure you I am not a witch. And if I brought a black cat in here, or any type of cat in here, Edgar over there would dive down and scratch it to ribbons."

"The bird seems to occupy the role of your familiar, as it were," said Holmes.

"My goodness, no, I hate him," she said. "But as long as I live here, so will he; I doubt I could ever get him to move. I despair at ever finding a husband."

"Did you see or hear anything on the day of the vandalism?" asked Holmes.

"I'm afraid I was visiting friends on that day. I can give you their details. Edgar was here; you can ask him. A few days earlier, I did see a couple of men hanging round with some kind of crate. Odd. It's a shame; poor Mr. Gossamer was a nice fellow. You will give him my best wishes, I hope?"

"What about Mr. and Mrs. Kelley?" asked Holmes.

"Well, I don't like to talk behind anyone's backs, but they are constantly at odds. It was even worse around that time; they would have enormous, loud arguments! I would almost have said it was about a baby, but their daughter is grown up and married, and they are hardly of age for another."

Mr. Kelley was not at home, and Mrs. Kelley would not speak to us, saying it wouldn't be proper, instead suggesting we went to talk to her husband at Manchester Zoological Gardens. We arrived and found him at the leopard enclosure.

"Gentlemen, I suggest you remain outside the cage, lest Pandora decide you are a predator or prey," he said ominously.

Once we explained why we were there, he immediately began berating Miss Barrington.

"You come to ask me about a black cat when there's a witch living right on our street? Mr. Holmes, you have a flair for missing the obvious."

"You believe she cursed Mr. Gossamer?" asked Holmes.

"I didn't say that," said Kelley, throwing raw meat to the leopard. "The man was a loon. I think he might have smashed his own windows, done those daubings. If he lost his job and his house, it was his own doing. Look at me; these gardens have come close to ruin several times due to lack of visitors, and I've rolled my sleeves up and provided. You make your own luck."

As we left the zoo, Holmes clapped his hands together.

"Mr. Kelley is absolutely right. And luckily, I know exactly who targeted Mr. Gossamer."

Question: Who does Sherlock Holmes think vandalized Mr. Gossamer's house?

Hint: Soot.

43   The Anti-Grail

" **T**his is not a police file," said Holmes, examining a manuscript. "It is a story about Camelot."

"Evidence from a crime? Or here by accident."

"No, it holds some other purpose," he said. "It's not one of the original tales. Ordinarily Arthur's knights seek the Grail to heal him. Not here. I think I know the author."

I reproduce the story here for you. Its greater significance will become apparent later...

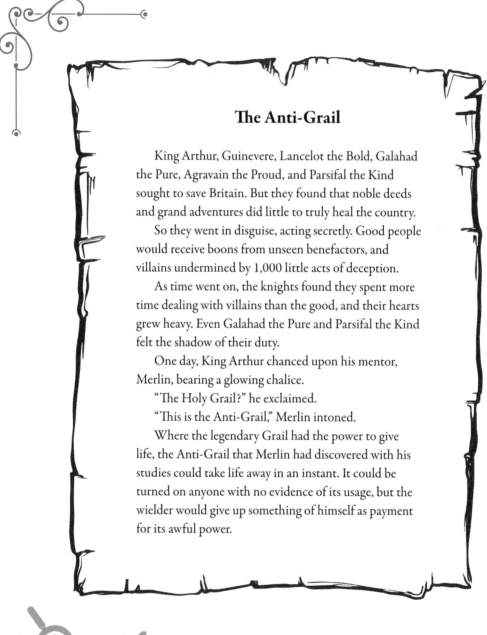

The Anti-Grail

King Arthur, Guinevere, Lancelot the Bold, Galahad the Pure, Agravain the Proud, and Parsifal the Kind sought to save Britain. But they found that noble deeds and grand adventures did little to truly heal the country.

So they went in disguise, acting secretly. Good people would receive boons from unseen benefactors, and villains undermined by 1,000 little acts of deception.

As time went on, the knights found they spent more time dealing with villains than the good, and their hearts grew heavy. Even Galahad the Pure and Parsifal the Kind felt the shadow of their duty.

One day, King Arthur chanced upon his mentor, Merlin, bearing a glowing chalice.

"The Holy Grail?" he exclaimed.

"This is the Anti-Grail," Merlin intoned.

Where the legendary Grail had the power to give life, the Anti-Grail that Merlin had discovered with his studies could take life away in an instant. It could be turned on anyone with no evidence of its usage, but the wielder would give up something of himself as payment for its awful power.

The knights were divided. King Arthur, Guinevere, Merlin, and Parsifal the Kind said it must never be used; mere man should not have ultimate power over life and death. However, Lancelot the Bold, Galahad the Pure, and Agravain the Proud said they must use it, as it was a divine gift that would allow them to truly rid Britain of villainy in secret.

The Anti-Grail remained in Merlin's possession. Until one day, Merlin was found dead. The powerful, ancient sorcerer could only have been killed by someone wielding the Grail.

King Arthur, horrified, sensed that it must have been Lancelot the Bold, Galahad the Pure, or Agravain the Proud.

He visited each of them. When he went to Lancelot the Bold's quarters, he saw that his faithful friend's hair had begun to turn silver at the temples.

"When I learned of our friend Merlin's horrible death, it chilled me to my soul," said Lancelot the Bold. "I have faced many terrible things in our time, but for Merlin, the reputed son of a literal demon, to be struck down so easily, I am sorry to say it has inspired a fear in me like no other. We must find the one who has done this and make them pay!"

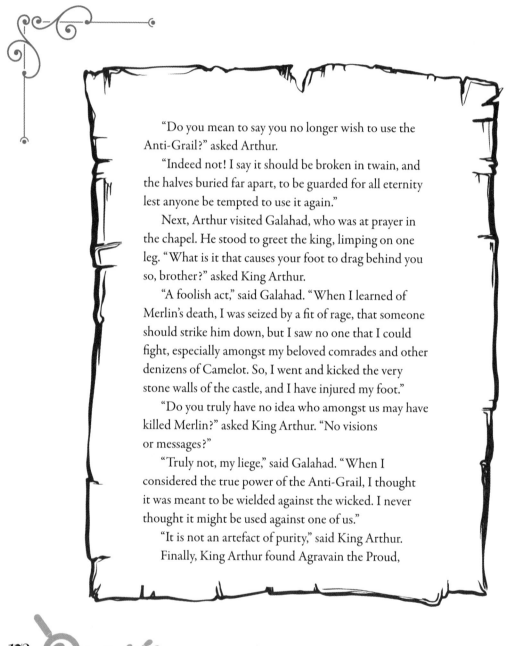

"Do you mean to say you no longer wish to use the Anti-Grail?" asked Arthur.

"Indeed not! I say it should be broken in twain, and the halves buried far apart, to be guarded for all eternity lest anyone be tempted to use it again."

Next, Arthur visited Galahad, who was at prayer in the chapel. He stood to greet the king, limping on one leg. "What is it that causes your foot to drag behind you so, brother?" asked King Arthur.

"A foolish act," said Galahad. "When I learned of Merlin's death, I was seized by a fit of rage, that someone should strike him down, but I saw no one that I could fight, especially amongst my beloved comrades and other denizens of Camelot. So, I went and kicked the very stone walls of the castle, and I have injured my foot."

"Do you truly have no idea who amongst us may have killed Merlin?" asked King Arthur. "No visions or messages?"

"Truly not, my liege," said Galahad. "When I considered the true power of the Anti-Grail, I thought it was meant to be wielded against the wicked. I never thought it might be used against one of us."

"It is not an artefact of purity," said King Arthur.

Finally, King Arthur found Agravain the Proud,

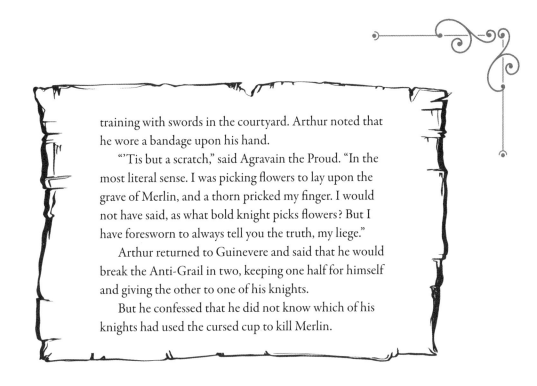

training with swords in the courtyard. Arthur noted that he wore a bandage upon his hand.

"'Tis but a scratch," said Agravain the Proud. "In the most literal sense. I was picking flowers to lay upon the grave of Merlin, and a thorn pricked my finger. I would not have said, as what bold knight picks flowers? But I have foresworn to always tell you the truth, my liege."

Arthur returned to Guinevere and said that he would break the Anti-Grail in two, keeping one half for himself and giving the other to one of his knights.

But he confessed that he did not know which of his knights had used the cursed cup to kill Merlin.

"A strange ending," I said. "But I suppose you know who did."

"I do, but only because the story's author did," said Holmes. "If you read it carefully it is easy to tell which of them lost something of themselves..."

Question: Who does Sherlock Holmes think killed Merlin in the story?

Hint: Missing word.

44. The Fortunate Hat

Eighteen months ago, Inspector Hallett of the Liverpool City Police purchased a hat from McClackerty & Son. Once home, he looked inside the hat and found, tucked into the inside band, a winning betting slip from Aintree Racecourse.

"It stuck out clearly, spotted it immediately. I despise gambling. I asked the milliners if it had been left by accident, but was shouted off the premises by Mr. McClackerty. I remembered that my hat had blown off after I'd left the shop, and a young lad had retrieved it, asking for a shilling. I said I was police, so he handed it over."

"You spoke to him again?" asked Holmes.

"Yes. He said his mother would hit him if she thought he'd been gambling. Between an angry hat-maker and this boy's mother, I decided to put an A on the file and forget it."

"Between the hat shop and your house, did anyone else touch your hat?" asked Holmes.

"No. Except my wife; she customarily takes my hat when I enter the house. But surely you can't suspect her?" he said.

The inspector unhappily summoned his wife, Mavis.

"Do you remember that day?" asked Holmes.

"It is difficult to forget," said Mrs. Hallett. "It's not often anyone would find that inside their hat, especially Alf! I hope you forgive me, but I briefly thought he had been gambling, and was claiming the slip was someone else's so he could collect the winnings. It would have helped with our budget. But he's an honest man."

"What was his reaction?" asked Holmes.

"Confusion? Annoyance? We don't often talk when he returns home as he has a long, tiring day, and he was late because he'd passed that funeral procession; he always pays his respects."

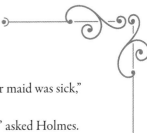

"Where were you during that day?" asked Holmes.

"At home, cleaning the whole house myself from top to bottom. Our maid was sick," she said sourly.

"Who do you think may have been responsible for what happened?" asked Holmes.

"I greatly admire my husband's abstemiousness, but it has made him a slight figure of fun amongst his fellow policemen, so perhaps one of them did it as a sort of jape?" she said.

We next located the milliners, McClackerty & Sons. Even with the passage of two years, the owner, Kier McClackerty, seemed incandescent over Inspector Hallett's suggestion.

"The nerve of that fellow. Calling himself an officer of the law!" he said with force. "I sell him an excellent black derby and he returns saying I put a betting slip inside. I organize a weekly meeting of men dedicated to eradicating the scourge of gambling from this city and he tries to smear my name. A hat from my shop shall ne'er again adorn his head!"

"I believe he was merely investigating the situation rather than pointing the finger," said Holmes. "Do you make your own hats? Who might have had access to them?"

"They are handmade in our workshop by myself and my three sons," said Mr. McClackerty. "And I assure you they are all reliable lads who also attend my meetings and would not gamble. And if they did, they would not risk the consequences of putting a ticket into one of our hats."

I thought Holmes might ask further about these assistants, but he had something else on his mind. We finally located the young man who had retrieved the hat, a 10-year-old boy named George Steptoe, and he seemed much happier than Mr. McClackerty.

"Please tell Inspector whatshisface I am extremely sorry I gave him such a cheek," Master Steptoe said. "I was very young, and I thought getting his hat back was such a feat it was worth a shilling. And then when he was talking about betting slips, I was worried, because my mother gave my dad such a thump when she found out he'd spent the coal money on a nag the winter before."

"And you didn't see a betting slip inside the hat when you gave it to him?" asked Holmes.

"No, but then I wasn't really looking very hard," the boy said. "Was it tucked it very tightly?"

"No, it was quite large and obvious. Why did his hat blow off?" asked Holmes.

"Well, I don't know if you've heard of it, but there's this thing called the wind," said the boy, and then he clapped his hand over his mouth before removing it. "Terribly sorry, Mr. Holmes. Cheek again. Truth is I love chasing things. It's lucky I got it when I did, as I nearly ran in front of the horses in that funeral procession."

We left the boy and headed back toward the inspector's house.

"The answer's clear, Watson. I am reluctant to reveal the culprit, as it will mean an uncomfortable conversation with a family member..."

Question: Who does Sherlock Holmes suspect put the betting slip in the hat?

Hint: Respect for the dead.

Level Two Cases

Introduction

In the past few weeks, as we had worked through the Anathema Archive files, I sensed there was some hidden motivation to Holmes' actions.

Then, one morning, he sent a message asking me to meet him at the rooms of his elder brother, Mycroft. Unlike his younger, slimmer sibling, Mycroft was a sedentary creature of almost unbreakable habits and left his rooms in Pall Mall only to visit his office in Whitehall and The Diogenes Club, moving between them like clockwork.

Mycroft's mind was supposedly superior to that of Sherlock, and while he gave the impression of being a mere functionary in Whitehall, in Holmes' words, "occasionally he is the British government."

Holmes led me into the rooms to show me, lying between two armed guards and a small group of doctors, his brother, apparently comatose in bed.

"He has been like this for about a month," said Holmes sharply. "Unresponsive, does not react to any kind of stimuli, heartbeat slow and weak. His blood shows no sign of any toxins or poisons."

Mycroft's mind worked like an enormous database of government business, both known and clandestine. Without him, they must be struggling.

A sharply dressed man with a warm smile stepped forward, extending his hand.

"Brendan Keoneen," he said dramatically. "We guard our secrets here with ferocity, but the stability of the entire world is at stake. So we had to initiate Mycroft's brother into the conspiracy."

"Only because you needed me to investigate this," said Holmes, showing me a slip of paper, on which was written, "MYCROFT'S SALVATION LIES IN THE ANATHEMA ARCHIVE."

"It was found on his desk next to his comatose body. Mr. Michaels wanted me to pursue this lead and gave me complete discretion. But neither of us realized the true

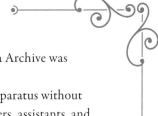

significance of this message. You see, I now know that the Anathema Archive was created by Mycroft himself."

"Yes, somehow he had funded and recruited an entire shadow apparatus without our knowledge," said Keoneen tetchily. "It seems a network of cleaners, assistants, and general dogsbodies secretly work for the Archive and spirit away anything marked with an A to the basement of this 'Mrs. Grabber.'"

"Yes, she seems to be the overseer of the whole operation," said Holmes. "And yesterday she passed me a letter that it seems Mycroft intended me to have should my actions somehow endanger the operation of the Archive itself."

He passed me the letter and I read it. Amongst all the dry technical details, a paragraph stood out:

"You seem to think extraordinary crimes need to be exposed to the light. I understand, from my experiences, that they should be banished to the dark. You dash around 'deducing' the solutions to crimes that to the average person seem incredible, while your own personal Boswell, Dr. Watson, records the encounters for the public to read. You say your example will lead to greater ingenuity in law enforcement. I say it is just creating more ingenious criminals. They get ideas from these tales or see mistakes that they can avoid. I created the Archive so that these mysteries could remain mysterious, their methods of execution a tool kept from the hands of others."

"When I was first told of Mycroft's malady, I was asked by Mr. Keoneen not to inform you of the full situation, for reasons of national security," said Holmes. "Once I had read Mycroft's letter, I realize now how wrong I was to keep you in the dark. Now that Mr. Keoneen knows that it was Mycroft who founded the Archive, we have agreed to reveal the truth to you so that you can assist me in finding his poisoner. Because he has been poisoned, I am sure of it, by something we cannot yet detect. And we are running out of time."

45 The Corn Dollies

This case was in fact three cases, each ten years apart, all telling a similar tale.

In 1872, Dr. Paul Horace, a fellow of St. Maximus College, Cambridge, died of a heart attack. His colleagues reported he'd been raving about a corn dolly left on his desk. He claimed it had supernatural powers. Dr. Horace was a Doctor of Medicine and had been published extensively debunking medical superstitions.

His fellows were surprised by his change of personality and subsequent demise.

The police tested him for substances and found nothing out of the ordinary (although opium was considered ordinary, I noted). They tested the dinner he had, the tableware, and many other objects, with no sign of poison. They also tested the corn dolly and found nothing. The investigator suppressed the case to prevent the press and public obsessing over it. Somehow, the dolly disappeared.

In 1882, the dolly, or a duplicate, appeared on the desk of Professor Stephen Taunton, chair of linguistics at St. Maximus. The professor had heard some of the "legend," but still displayed it by his inkwell.

Days later, he was seen in a similar state to Dr. Horace, proclaiming the dolly cursed, and despite attempts at an intervention, died soon after.

The new investigator tested everything in Horace's residence and workplace for poison, to no avail, and once again the dolly was also clean, as was the professor's blood.

"In 1892 I was 'dead,' otherwise I may have investigated this sooner," said Holmes. "Five years ago, a Professor of Philosophy named Clive Nix, also at St. Maximus, found a dolly. Sensibly he contacted the police, then admitted himself to a hospital for tests. Clean bill. He released himself, then several days later ended up raving about the dolly's dark spirit and dying. However, this time they did find something in his blood, using a technique I devised. An unidentified toxin."

"Clearly no curse, then," I said. "Like the hound."

"As with the Baskervilles, there is a dark spirit behind this, a human one."

Holmes said that the only connection between the men, other than the doll and St. Maximus, was that they were all highly successful. Each had been considered remarkably knowledgeable, and therefore people whispered that the "straw doll's curse" was a supernatural punishment for their own hubris.

"The Archive really struggled to suppress it this time; the newspapers were practically salivating at the story," said Holmes. "Not only because of the repeated nature of this mysterious crime and the high profile of the victims, but the supernatural element."

Holmes explained that the college had been built on land formerly farmed by a wild clan of locals called the Meeks. When the lord who owned the land turned it over to the college and had the Meeks evicted, they swore revenge. Every time a member of the lord's family died, a Meek would say it was their revenge, but foul play was never suspected or even likely as the Meeks tended to live up to their own surname when it came to threats.

"The only remaining member is Isobel Meek, a septuagenarian who lives in a cottage in the fenlands. She's a hermit, but has been known to venture into the town to sell poultices, folk charms, and... corn dollies."

I tried not to react. Holmes smiled wryly.

"Watson, you practically jumped out of your seat when I said that. We will be speaking to Mrs. Meek, as well as the only other two people who have been at St. Maximus from 1872 to 1892."

Considering the stagnation of Cambridge colleges, I found this surprising, but it was true from this 25-year period that the only two people who had never left the college were Harold Coppice, a history student who became a professor, and Eustace Raynott, the head librarian.

We found Coppice in a local pub, sipping ale.

"The study of history is disappointing. Your fantasies of great battles and noble kings end up revealing the pettiness of humanity," he said.

"Your view of the victims?" asked Holmes.

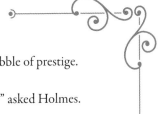

"No! I was indifferent. They didn't know I existed, moving in a bubble of prestige. Along with most of the money."

"In 1872, you were a student. Do you remember the first incident?" asked Holmes.

Coppice livened up.

"When the dolly turned up on Horace's desk, the Fellows stalked around the building. They wanted to find the culprit. Horace was an encyclopaedia of medical facts, but knew next to nothing about non-medical history."

"How did he conclude it was cursed?" I asked. "Someone told him?"

"Not the other fellows," Coppice said. "They were as logical as him. One of the students? Our brains were full of history, not folklore. Perhaps he did some research?"

"Corn dollies aren't traditionally cursed objects," said Holmes.

"Really?" said Coppice. "We all knew the stories about the Meeks. Sometimes I'd see that old lady Meek in town."

Holmes asked him about Stephen Taunton.

"A chancer," said Coppice bitterly. "Framed himself as a traditionalist. But his 'intelligence' was carefully rehearsed."

"He wasn't afraid of the dolly?"

"No, he loved the macabre. We'd been told never to mention any of the things Horace had said. When he started shouting the same things, we thought someone must have blabbed. 'It's cursed, I read it!' Then he died."

"Any enemies?" I asked.

"Plenty. But they needed him; they moved in his wake."

"What of Clive Nix?"

"Didn't know him," he said quickly. "I was dealing with some challenging students at that time. I knew his reputation. When I heard he'd been hospitalized, I thought it might have been overeating. I was as surprised to find him charging down the corridor screaming about the curse like the first two."

"Did they know Eustace Raynott?" asked Holmes.

"Who?"

"The head librarian."

"Oh, him. Don't know. I saw them going in a few times. Raynott's odd. He cornered me a couple of times, trying to lecture me about some subject. After that, I'd steer clear."

Harold Coppice was downbeat but willing to talk. Eustace Raynott was the opposite, energetic for an octogenarian, but with little time to waste on our enquiries.

His library had the books ranked in neat rows with no gaps, although that might indicate that few visited.

"I was told I was not to discuss the corn dolly nonsense," he said, pushing a trolley with a couple of books.

"You may speak freely," said Holmes.

"But I don't know anything about what happened," said Raynott.

"Did you know the victims?" Holmes asked as Raynott climbed a ladder, pushing a slim volume about French mythology into a much wider gap.

"Since 1854, countless fellows have used this library. I chose to remember the books under my care rather than faces."

"Yes or no?" said Holmes sharply.

Raynott stopped filing.

"I knew 'of' them. The first chap, Horace, was here when I started. Can't remember the second one's name, but he came from Oxford, big brouhaha about that."

"And Nix?" interrupted Holmes.

Raynott pursed his lips. "A former student here, went away and returned. I know about many subjects, but none of these men came into this library."

"What about the corn dolly?"

Raynott shook his head emphatically.

"This is a library dedicated to facts. When the college displaced that sinister Meek family, it was a metaphorical tide of reason washing away the dregs of superstition from this area."

"Myths and legends provide insights into the mind that science and philosophy fail to grasp," said Holmes.

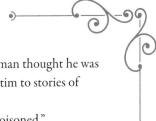

"I agree," said Raynott. "It's the key to these deaths: hysteria. Each man thought he was of steady mind. But their studies were superficial, so they could fall victim to stories of curses. Then they died from stress."

"Scared to death?" I said suspiciously. "We know at least one was poisoned."

"Hm, really? Possibly death by suicide, then," said Raynott.

Miss Meek's cottage defied my expectations as it was well-kept with a small garden.

Isobel Meek, though clearly old, didn't match the description we'd received.

"You mean the mystical robes? That's just for when I go into town," she said. "For tourists. I doubt locals would recognize me without them."

"You've worked as a cleaner at St. Maximus for 29 years?" asked Holmes.

Instead of showing surprise, Miss Meek smiled and invited us inside.

The interior had a few magical-looking books and items around, with a corn dolly on the table.

"No one noticed me," she said. "I took the job under a false name to try and find information. It was decent money, especially as the call for folk magic waxes and wanes."

"Is this...?" I queried, pointing at the corn dolly on the table.

"The cursed object? No. The first dolly, that was me. That old goat was constantly slighting 'folk remedies' so I hid it in his office as a joke. Where he got the idea it had a curse, I don't know."

"And Stephen Taunton and Clive Nix?"

"Taunton had muddy boots; Nix left dirty plates. If you mean the dollies, they weren't mine. Someone could have bought one and used it. All corn dollies look the same. They looked just as puzzled as Dr. Howard, and as ignorant about folk history."

"Do you know Harold Coppice, or Eustace Raynott?" asked Holmes.

"Of course. I doubt they know me!" she said. "Harold's not meant for academia. But nice enough. Raynott's the reverse, a good librarian but hates it. He had to leave another college in disgrace over something. Always lecturing everyone, even bright stars like Taunton and Nix."

"What do you think killed all these people?" I asked her.

"Poison," she said frankly. "Some mushrooms turn you doolally before you die. But where's the benefit for me? I didn't get our land back."

Outside, Holmes said thoughtfully, "She did benefit. The deaths must have driven the trade in her remedies and spells."

"But driven down the sale of corn dollies?" I suggested. "Would Coppice kill them from his own jealousy? Or did they wrong Raynott somehow? Maybe they licked their fingers to turn pages, or bend the book's spines the wrong way..."

"Ah, Watson. Ignorance can be deadly, yet so can knowledge, depending on how it is received."

Question: Who does Holmes know killed Dr. Howard, Professor Taunton, and Professor Nix?

Hints: The men were not as intelligent as they seemed.
There is a primary source of information in the story.
One suspect's statement disagrees with the other two.
There is an object not mentioned in the story that all three men touched.

46 The Invisible Knight

"It's Haukwood with a 'u,'" said Holmes as we journeyed to the Hampshire village of that name. "These villagers are very insistent on spellings, even though 200 years ago people spelled their names 20 different ways..."

The village was proud of its medieval connections, with its 650-year-old church, St. George's-in-the-fields, and its statue of Sir John Haukwood on his horse.

The statue lay at the heart of a mysterious murder that happened two years previously. A local landowner died with no heir, and his property was bought by a London businessman, Montgomery Hoggett. He planned to raze the land he'd bought and use it as a rubbish tip for his factories. This outraged the locals.

Real trouble began when he broke the statue. His carriage was going too fast, and his coachman failed to take a corner, colliding with the statue of Sir John Haukwood at speed. Hoggett stumbled out, laughing.

The villagers gathered round, and Victoria Chesham, the parish clerk, after inspecting the broken statue, loudly lambasted Hoggett.

When Hoggett stepped toward Miss Chesham in a threatening manner, Seth Hawkwood (landlord of the local pub, The Sir John's Steed) stepped between them and gave the businessman "a look of burning hatred." Hoggett and his uninjured coachman sought the protection of the local police.

After this, Hoggett would walk around town provoking the locals. For protection, he arranged for two heavily armed Pinkerton agents from America to act as bodyguards.

One day, Hoggett was having tea at the house of Tarquin Vandemeer, local stable owner. Vandemeer remarked that someone had written something critical of Hoggett in a narrow passageway in the village. Incensed, Hoggett and his bodyguards went there immediately.

"Hoggett positioned a bodyguard at each end of the passageway and went to examine the message," said Holmes. "The Pinkertons say that they were both turned away from him when they heard a cry. They turned back to see he had been stabbed through the stomach by a sword, dying immediately! No one was seen entering or exiting the passageway, and witnesses at either end testified that the Pinkertons didn't move from their positions. Remarkably, the sword that killed Hoggett was the one formerly held by the statue of Sir John that he had destroyed!"

"Any other evidence?"

"None. Not even footprints," said Holmes. "There were suspects. Seth Hawkwood hated Hoggett for his actions toward the village and his supposed ancestor. He was strong and tall enough to have made the killing blow. Victoria Chesham's hatred was stronger, though she would have struggled to have lifted the sword. Hoggett's 'friend' Tarquin Vandemeer had expressed his distaste for the rubbish tip being built next to his stables. He bought Hoggett's land after the murder. One of these villagers is our knight."

Arriving at 4 pm, we were met by Seth Hawkwood.

"Mr. Holmes, a pleasure!" he beamed, shaking his hand vigorously. Hawkwood was 6 foot 4, his strength evident when he shook my hand.

"My views on Hoggett were plain, but that doesn't mean I wanted him dead!" he declared as we strode toward the murder scene.

"You claim to have been in your public house at the time," said Holmes, taking note of the restored statue of Sir John.

"I was in The Sir John's Steed; five patrons can attest to that," Seth said.

"At 1:30 pm?" I asked.

"They are older gentlemen who have moved from the world of work to the world of..."

"Drinking?" suggested Holmes. "That may render their testimony unreliable."

Seth looked scandalized. "They are church-going men of good character. Ah, here we are."

The passageway was narrow, barely enough room for two men. Holmes examined the entrance.

"Mr. Hawkwood, please remain here," he said, and indicated to me that we enter the passageway.

"There's only one door within this passage," he said, indicating a gnarled wooden door. "I've been reassured this is the oldest door in the village and hasn't opened for one hundred years because it's too warped."

I tried at pulling it open, but it was totally immovable. Holmes crouched.

"There's no signs of sewer grates or other kinds of subterranean access."

A message was carved into the stone of the north-facing wall. It read: "HAUKWOOD SHALL NEVER BECOME HOGGWOOD."

"Hoggett stations his men at either end, walks here to look at the message, then within seconds he's transfixed by Sir John's sword! The killer leaves no footprints. In fact, they would have barely enough room to stand in front of him and strike this blow."

We exited the other end to find Seth standing there.

"Are people sure he entered the alleyway at all?" I asked. "It's quite dark."

"Ah, that's the shadow of the church tower," said Seth, pointing south to the belfry. "It was 1:30 pm in July when Hoggett was stabbed, so the alley would have been as clear and bright as the sound of St. George's bells..."

Holmes asked Hawkwood about the other suspects, but he was dismissive of the idea that Tarquin Vandemeer could have done it; as several grooms testified, he'd been at his stables miles away. Hawkwood openly laughed at the suggestion Miss Chesham could have done it, performing a mime of a tiny woman trying to lift the large sword.

Miss Chesham may have been short, but I wouldn't describe her as weak; when we arrived at St. George's-in-the-fields, the bells were ringing with incredible enthusiasm, and she was the only person pulling the ropes!

"With you in a tick!" she shouted as we climbed into the belltower. She finished the peal and came over, red-faced. She stood just under 5 foot and curtsied to Holmes, who was looking down from the belltower to the alleyway.

"You were bell-ringing at the time of the murder. Are you sure you didn't see anything?" asked Holmes.

"When I'm bell-ringing, I can't concentrate on anything but the changes. It's hard work," she said.

"You have no assistance?" I asked.

"Reverend Barnaby, and the verger, Bill Jones, are ringers. Sometimes Seth Hawkwood has a go, although he's uncoordinated. That day, I was alone as everyone was gawking at Hoggett's Pinkertons. The reverend and verger can confirm I was up here; they saw me ascend and there's no other way to descend. Everyone heard me ringing the bells."

"You must have been glad to see Hoggett dead," said Holmes.

"How can you say something like that in a church, Mr. Holmes? It's true that Hoggett's fate lay in his own hands. He disrespected this village, its people, its traditions, and most importantly, Sir John himself. No good woman would be glad he died. But I was not surprised, either."

"Do you think Seth Hawkwood could have killed him? Or Tarquin Vandemeer?" I asked.

"Mr. Vandemeer, I don't know. He's not a churchgoer, and he seemed very friendly with Hoggett before the incident. But if you speak ill of Seth here once again, I shall ask you to leave."

"What do you think happened?" Holmes asked. She seemed surprised he would ask her opinion.

"All I know is when the statue was destroyed, I could feel Sir John's restless spirit in the village. After he died, that feeling passed."

It was getting dark, so we set off to Vandemeer's stables, stopping on the way to visit Constable Nobbs, who'd found the murder weapon. The constable presented it to us like it was Excalibur.

"Sir John's sword," he said reverently. "They wanted it back when they rebuilt the statue, but I couldn't allow evidence to leave the station."

"Though you were happy to send the case to the Anathema Archive," Holmes remarked, to the constable's shame. Holmes picked up the sword.

"Hmm, lighter than I thought," he remarked. "Iron, but perhaps hollow? And this cross guard is unusual," indicating its fin-like shapes. Looking at the end of the pommel, he showed me there was a cross indentation on the bottom.

Holmes took the sword with him to the stables; when we arrived, Vandemeer's butler showed us into the great hall. Vandemeer was remarkably fit for a man in his sixties. Roughly 6 foot 1, but I noticed that his boots had thicker soles than usual. Was he self-conscious of his height?

"Hoggett was a ruthless man, used to getting his own way. I admired that, even if he planned on turning the countryside into a cesspit. I tried to help him understand the people here were good, noble, but he'd decided they were obstacles."

"Do you have much contact with them? Miss Chesham said you're not a churchgoer?" said Holmes.

"I don't often venture down into Haukwood, but I host the midsummer festival here and everyone attends, especially her."

"This is the festival of medieval activities. Jousting, swordfights, archery?" said Holmes.

"Miss Chesham is the best archer in the village, although I wouldn't mention that to Seth Hawkwood; he fancies himself as Robin Hood. She preferred the crossbow, to let Seth be longbow champion. It's wise to be his friend; it opens doors round here."

"Does Hawkwood do any sword fighting?" Holmes asked.

"Oh, indeed! Seth can wield a blade with great alacrity! He even bested me a time or two. Victoria Chesham has never had a sword fight in her life. Those bell-ringer's arms would have stood her in good stead, but she's not the type to stab a person."

"Would you, Mr. Vandemeer?" asked Holmes.

Vandemeer considered this. "I have witnesses that I was here in the stables when Hoggett was killed. I'm not superstitious, but the church bells seemed to pause for a moment at the time he was skewered."

We walked out into the night and Holmes filled his pipe. "The solution is now clear to me. A fantastic crime, certainly… and far from a chivalrous one."

Question: Who does Sherlock Holmes suspect killed Montgomery Hoggett?

Hints: Not much room for two in the corridor.
The corridor can see the belltower and vice versa.
The sword is shaped strangely.
A blade need not be held to be used.

$\text{\scriptsize 47}$ The Broken Mask

I didn't recognize the face before me, but recognized the expression: the cold, slackened countenance of a body whose soul has departed. A death mask. Rendered in plaster, with large cracks dividing it into five pieces.

Thirteen years ago, five robberies were committed in five different places across England. Ruislip, Nuneaton, Hythe, Biddisham, and Ealing in London. All people from different walks of life. No connection between the crimes, save for three things: firstly, the robberies had been executed via upper floor windows, suggesting a nimble, skilled individual. Secondly, the victims had visited London that year. Thirdly, at each location the police had found a piece of the plaster mask.

"He's not one of ours, Watson," said Holmes as he leafed through an enormous folder he kept on the shelves. "I know the faces of everyone we've tangled with."

"Is that a face-book?" I asked him.

"No, this is one of my fingerprint files."

Holmes had thus far failed to convince Scotland Yard that they needed to keep a record of the fingerprints of criminals, so he collected them himself.

"I have dusted this mask and found three sets of fingerprints. All three sets belong to three individuals we have already met. Only one of them is a criminal. And none is a burglar."

The first belonged to Leonard Bright, a former hangman who was dismissed from his post for stealing. We had not solved that case, but had taken his prints to eliminate him from the Mathews Case.

The second fingerprints belonged to Humility McManus, a housewife whose prints we had taken to eliminate her when the cat next door had been poisoned, in the case of Old Abrahams.

The third belonged to David Gilbert, a bric-à-brac shop owner who had been suspected of handling various stolen goods, never successfully proven.

"If Bright is involved, this certainly seems to confirm my thoughts that this is a death mask, Holmes," I said.

"Yes, and no doubt you noticed the tiny threads at the bottom edge of the mask indicated this is the original, most likely made before the noose was removed from the man's neck," said Holmes.

"I'm sure I would have, given time," I said brusquely.

"We have no time, Watson, we must away," Holmes said, leaping up toward the door.

After his dismissal, Leonard Bright had become a public speaker against the sins of gambling and drinking. He credited them for his descent into criminality. He also regretted his own role in hanging so many men.

Bright didn't look happy to see us when we appeared at one of his lectures in a small hall in Redbridge.

"You have arrived a little too late to benefit from my talk, but perhaps I can offer you a pamphlet?" he said uneasily.

"No need, Mr. Bright, I simply need to ask your advice about this," Holmes said, laying the now repaired death mask on top of the pamphlets.

Bright's eyes widened, he turned pale, and his hands flew up as if to protect himself.

"W-where... did you get that?" he stammered.

"The pieces were found at the scene of five different burglaries," said Holmes, watching Bright's reaction. "Please do not insult us by pretending you didn't recognize it."

Bright nodded with regret.

"It's the death mask of Praise-God Darby." Holmes nodded.

"Of course."

"Who was he?" I asked Holmes.

"I'm surprised you missed the case Watson," said Holmes. "Praise-God Darby was born to a prosperous quaker family, hence the 'virtue name' typical to people of that group. But he disgraced them when he killed a love rival named Diffidence Allen. His case was in the

papers for months as the whole sordid affair was undone, but once he was convicted and executed press and public interest drifted."

Holmes touched the mask.

"Did you make it yourself, Mr Bright?" Holmes asked.

"We often made them," he said quickly. "For the family of the condemned."

"And did Praise-God Darby's family receive this mask?" asked Holmes.

"Well, no..." said Bright, cagily. "They distanced themselves from him as soon as the trial began."

"Who received it?"

"I don't know. It was misplaced, I think," said Bright, perspiring.

"Misplaced in the same way as the pocket watch you took from Gregory Hill?" said Holmes pointedly.

Bright hung his head low.

"Mr. Holmes, every day I regret when I stole that condemned man's watch.

I can say, honestly, that I don't know how pieces of the mask were placed into the people's houses."

On the journey back to London, Holmes said, "Note, Watson, that I did not say the pieces of the mask were left at the burglaries, merely found."

"It's not unusual to assume that items found after a burglary might be left by the burglar," I countered.

Humility McManus had not responded to our requests for an interview, but when Holmes suggested he might bring it up with Scotland Yard, she had quickly assented, at Holmes' residence away from prying eyes.

She was a short, plump lady whose tiny smile was betrayed by sad eyes. She perched on the edge of Holmes' armchair and fiddled with a hempen bracelet while Holmes explained about her fingerprints on the mask.

"I would have preferred thee had specified why thee needed to speak to me in the telegrams you sent," she said carefully. "I thought initially it was about the poisoned cat again."

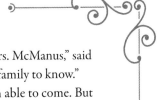

"I am not certain of the nature of your involvement in this case, Mrs. McManus," said Holmes. "We understood that you might not wish your husband and family to know."

"I was forced to tell my husband, otherwise I would not have been able to come. But he already knew about my interests," she said, glancing at the plaster mask on the table nearby. "When I was young and foolish, I had a strange fascination with criminals, Praise-God Darby in particular. Every detail of the story, every new broadsheet or pamphlet, I'd devour it."

"That's not unusual., I said comfortingly. "Everyone was fascinated."

She shook her head. "They shouldn't have been. It's pathetic. I even took to waiting outside the courthouse, trying to see him, or the jailers, anyone, like a vulture. That was no way for a Catholic girl to behave. When I heard he'd hang, I wept. Out of pity for myself, that I wouldn't see him again."

She paused, fiddling with that bracelet.

"I was in the crowd outside the day he hanged. They dispersed once his death was announced and I wept again, thinking of his life choking out of him. Leonard Bright caught my eye and beckoned me round the back. He showed me the death mask, let me touch it. Another jailer caught us, so I was able to run away before he could try anything; after that I was ashamed."

Holmes had sat rigid throughout this story; now he stood up.

"So you did not take the mask? Offer money for it?"

She shook her head fiercely. "Perhaps if we had not been disturbed, I would have."

"And the robberies, you know nothing about them?"

"Not at all," she said. "Are you sure that the mask pieces were not owned by the people?"

"It is not impossible," said Holmes. "But small details in the manner of the burglary in all five cases have suggested to me that they had to have been done by the same man."

"Well, I hope you catch him," she said with a small smile.

David Gilbert's bric-à-brac shop had the air of ten antiques stalls crammed into a single room.

As he entered, Holmes loudly remarked, "Such a dusty shop!"

If his intent was to irritate Mr. Gilbert, it had no effect.

"Mr. Holmes! A pleasure to see you again; apologies for the dustiness. My hands have been suffering lately from pains."

Holmes placed the mask onto the counter.

"What's this? Looks like a death mask. I'm afraid I won't deal in these items."

"Come now, Mr. Gilbert," said Holmes. "I found your fingerprints on this mask."

"You must be mistaken," Gilbert said.

I couldn't see this exchange, as I was in the alley behind the shop.

"You surprise me, Mr. Gilbert," Holmes said, which was my cue to smash Gilbert's back window. I heard Gilbert shout in alarm and immediately run to his back entrance and throw the door open.

"What is the meaning of this?" he shouted angrily.

"I thought I saw a suffocating peacock in there," I said.

"Watson, stop your ridiculous distraction and bring Mr. Gilbert through," Holmes said loudly from the shop. Gilbert turned and marched back in. I followed him through the surprisingly clean and empty stock room into the shop, where Holmes stood leafing through an old book.

"How dare you," Gilbert declared, and went to take the book. But as a stooped man looking twice his age, he was no match for Holmes who simply stepped backward.

"An interesting book, documenting roughly 21 years of sales. No items listed, merely payments and initials. And it stops 13 years ago."

He showed me the book.

"Look, Watson, in 1881 Mr. Gilbert sold 'H-MAC' for 19 shillings to an FK. Do you remember in 1884, we arrested a Mr. Frederick Katz and found he had a handkerchief purported to be owned by Mary Ann Cotton, the 'dark angel?' and perhaps the PS who you sold 'S-BH' to in 1879 was the Philip Solderman we caught trying to sell Burke and Hare's shovels in 1886."

Gilbert was reddening by the instant.

"This is slander!" He sputtered.

"I see a few DMs that may mean 'death mask,'" Holmes continued. "But no 'DM-PGD.' Interestingly, though, these five entries before the book concludes all bear the initials of the five people who were robbed."

"Give me that this instant!" Gilbert shouted.

Holmes showed me the entries for those people. Written next to them were "R-PGD."

Holmes dropped the book on the counter and strode out of the shop. As we walked down the street, he looked thoughtful despite Gilbert shouting threats behind us.

"I understand it now," he said. "There can be only one culprit. The robberies were not an act of greed, but of morality."

"Not Gilbert, then, surely," I said. "Selling all those items, he didn't care about the people they came from; a way to make easy profit. Money for old rope."

Holmes looked at me with the rare delight he receives when I have solved a mystery without his explanation... which confused me, as I still had no clue as to who was guilty.

Question: Who does Sherlock Holmes suspect committed the five burglaries?

Hints: Bright does not need to rob people to get artefacts.
Gilbert stopped selling these items around the time of the robbery.
Disrespect often breeds anger.
Families often have similar names.

48   The Lestrade Report

I, Inspector Lestrade, will detail herein my experience of the events surrounding the theft of Lady Merriweather's fan, my discovery of its location, my decision regarding the case's suppression, and what happened when this came to light.

Lady Merriweather, a well-respected widow of the parish of Kensington, summoned the police to her domicile on the evening of 16th of November 1895. A valuable fan had been stolen from the premises. She had seen it several hours earlier, suggesting the robbery had occurred that afternoon. The only people present at that time were servants (whose alibis were solid), her housekeeper Mrs. Elsie Arnold, the coal man Mr. Hollis Fairmane (who visited only the coal hole for approximately 23 minutes), and Mrs. A. Hudson, housekeeper of Mr. Sherlock Holmes, visiting her friend Mrs. Arnold for about 43 minutes.

After two days, I sought the counsel of Mr. Holmes. Although I find his methods scattershot, his deductive skills have been of great benefit to the Yard. I reacted with shock when I saw that the very fan Lady Merriweather had described (white, dark brown lacquer lining, motif of yellowhammer birds with irregular dot and dash pattern) was placed above the fireplace in Mr. Holmes' rooms.

I asked Mr. Holmes the origin of the fan. He responded as such:

"Oh, I don't know, Mrs. Hudson has taken to sneaking these little womanly touches around the place, to counteract what she calls my 'natural man's messiness.'"

Knowing Mrs. Hudson had been present at Lady Merriweather's house on the day in question, I concluded that she had stolen the fan from the house.

Lady Merriweather was an important woman. Furthermore, it would ill benefit Mr. Holmes' reputation to have a thief work for him. However, his help was essential for the ongoing success of Scotland Yard, and Mrs. Hudson was an excellent housekeeper, without whom Holmes' residence would descend into slobbish anarchy.

I made the decision not to inform Lady Merriweather of the fan's location, nor Mr. Holmes of his housekeeper's larceny, and instead marked the case with an A, knowing that this would mean it would be spirited away. I had therefore helped secure the conviction of dozens if not hundreds of future criminals.

Several months later, I was approached by Mr. Holmes regarding the matter of "The Anathema Archive," the self-same place that all files marked with an A are secreted to. I affected ignorance, then disbelief, and finally relented when he showed me an official document granting him permission to access the Archive. As I did not know its location, I informed him that he was welcome to go there if he could find it, hoping that this would be beyond even his skills.

Two weeks later, I pretended to casually drop by 221b Baker Street on non-police matters to see if Mr. Holmes had unearthed the file. He was elsewhere but Dr. John Watson was in residence, so I explained the situation, and my concern regarding the criminal nature of his housekeeper.

Dr. Watson questioned the reasoning of my conclusion vis-à-vis the purloined fan, suggesting that Mrs. Hudson deserved the assumption of innocence, and that I should tell Mr. Holmes the truth so that he could apply his own investigative skills.

In Dr. Watson's published accounts of their cases which featured myself, I was treated as if I was incapable of the most basic logical thought. People do not rise to the level that I have attained within Scotland Yard without being able to put two and two together.

I informed him that I would investigate it myself, and made him swear that he would not inform Mr. Holmes of this situation until I had reached my conclusion. He reluctantly agreed.

My first port of call was Mrs. Hudson herself, who currently toiled in the kitchens, scrubbing the stove. My efforts at small talk were treated with understandable confusion and a small amount of hostility, so I proceeded quickly to the subject of the fan. Mrs. Hudson's response was as follows:

"I haven't a clue, Mr. Lestrade. Mr. Holmes often has all kinds of unusual items strewn around and attached to his walls. On one occasion I found he had knocked a hole in the wall and stuffed it with doll's heads for whatever reason. Another time..."

I asked if she remembered visiting the house of Lady Merriweather.

"Oh yes, Elsie, Mrs. Arnold, had found a big mark on one of the lady's silver plates and knows I have a knack for getting rid of them. I don't mean to speak out of turn, but Lady Merriweather does not have a merry disposition at all; Mrs. Arnold is frequently forced to produce elaborate banquets at the drop of the hat."

I then employed a clever police technique, whereby I described the current situation but cloaked it as having happened to other unrelated individuals. I wove her a story about the housekeeper of a friend of mine visiting a different housekeeper and "borrowing" a teapot she took a fancy to, and pondered what consequences Mrs. Hudson thought appropriate.

"I didn't steal the fan, Mr. Lestrade, if that's what you're getting at, and I'd ask you to leave my kitchen at once and cease getting in the way of my work with unjustified accusations. Mrs. Arnold came over to Baker Street a day later; surely if it was the same fan, she would have said something!"

So, Mrs. Arnold had the opportunity to put the fan there herself? I decided to employ a different technique to question Elsie Arnold, as I did not want Lady Merriweather to know about my queries, so I visited the household under the pretence of investigating a series of burglaries in the area. I brought up the subject of the fan quite naturally, and once I gave her my solemn oath, she could speak frankly and provided some insight:

"She made such a fuss about that for a long time, and not her usual fuss like when she loses some earrings; this was more like when I accidentally dusted that safe in her room. She kept saying she needed to get it back, like she'd be in trouble. Then all of a sudden, she tells us we're never to mention it again or we'll be sacked. Then I see her late one night whispering to these two rough-looking men over by the coal hole."

Regarding the coal hole, I asked if she had any doubts about the integrity of Hollis Fairmane, the coal man.

"Oh, maybe. But not to steal anything. He was covered in coal dust; there'd be smudges everywhere. But he was bad at his job; he must've been slinging the coal in there very hard to make such a hole in the wall. He lost all his business when that man said he'd dragged

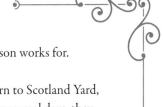

dirty coal sacks all through his corridor. That skinny fellow Mrs. Hudson works for. Although I visited there, and I didn't see anything on the carpet."

Hollis Fairmane now seemed like a viable suspect as well. On return to Scotland Yard, I directed several officers to locate Mr. Fairmane for questioning. After several days, they informed me that they could find no trace, nor evidence of his business.

I decided I would have to surreptitiously question Mr. Holmes, as he was the only other person who had been confirmed to hire Fairmane. This would be my ultimate challenge, as I had to somehow extract this information from him without him realizing the truth about the fan, or Mrs. Hudson's potential criminal nature.

I decided instead to tell him everything.

"Mrs. Hudson is some kind of master burglar? Clap her in irons immediately, Inspector!"

I pointed out that I merely believed she had been seized by a fit of jealousy and had grabbed the fan without thinking. I asked him what he thought.

"You might be onto something with this Fairmane fellow, Lestrade. His bonafides seemed fine to Mrs. Hudson when she needed a new coal man, but he clearly had no idea what he was actually doing. If, as you say, he has no apparent footprint on the world of workmen, I dare say he was some kind of imposter, or perhaps never existed at all."

I asked if Mr. Holmes was suggesting Fairmane was the agent of some malefactor, perhaps one of Moriarty's crew.

"The tool of a mastermind. Yes, I think you're onto something there, I think that's exactly what he is. Or was. I suggest you step back from this for now. And please return the lady's fan, although don't yet divulge its origins."

He gave me the fan and I decided I would return it. As I made my way to Lady Merriweather's house, I considered the facts.

Mr. Holmes made a strong case for Hollis Fairmane having been the thief, but was he simply dissembling to further protect Mrs. Hudson?

Why did he discount the potential guilt of Elsie Arnold? Was it because she reminded him too much of Mrs. Hudson, or was Mr. Holmes once again underestimating the possibility of a female criminal?

Why did I not mention to Mr. Holmes that I had noticed that he had done various drawings of the fan, particularly its unusual, lined pattern, and marked them with what looked like letters and numbers? Was it because I was reluctant to admit that his lessons of deduction and observation had ultimately rubbed off on me?

When I returned the fan to Lady Merriweather, she tried to hide her relief, but her eyes showed it. She made it clear I should leave immediately, but I then carefully hung around nearby to observe; sure enough, two surly looking gentlemen matching the description Mrs. Arnold gave arrived later. Lady Merriweather stood in the shadows, handing them the fan, and I became aware of a presence behind me, the presence of the fan's original thief. I am glad to report that I did manage to put two and two together and came up with one.

Question: Who does Inspector Lestrade suspect stole Lady Merriweather's fan?

Hints: Hollis Fairmane only had two employers.
Lady Merriweather was extremely worried about getting the fan back.
The fan has interesting markings on it.
Would Holmes really have anything in his study of which he was unaware?

49 The Ticker Man

"When you hear the Ticker Man's tick tick tick,
You'd better try to find him quick quick quick,
Or I'll put you in a sack, and I'll beat you with a stick,
And I'll throw you in the Thames with a brick brick brick."

A boy and girl were singing this rhyme as we entered the
courtyard of Wormelow House in Knightsbridge.

Holmes asked where they had learned it.

"Don't know," said the boy.

"I heard it from Susan; apparently she heard it from
Colin," said the older girl. "They don't come to lessons
anymore."

"It's true," said the boy. "You hear his ticking inside the
house. Adults never hear it, but it's there."

This was both welcome and horrifying news.

Fifteen years ago, three scientific institutions were bombed,
causing three deaths and 12 injuries. The detonation at the third site was only partially
successful, so investigators were able to recover evidence of the time-bomb.

"Remarkable design. The sophisticated clockwork and spring meant that once
wound, it could remain active for decades," said Holmes. "The perpetrator and
intention of the bombings remained unknown, but most concerningly, there was a
fourth bomb."

Holmes was able to deduce the existence of a fourth bomb from gaps in the
available data within the case file. He traced the first three as having been mailed from

an address in Piccadilly, rented under a false name. The fourth bomb had been sent to the wrong place in error: Wormelow House, rather than the Warmelow Institute of Chemical Engineering.

"No explosion or bomb was reported. Either the bomber recovered their package, or it remains there, undiscovered, potentially about to explode," said Holmes grimly.

"But why would the bomber even care to retrieve it?" I asked.

"They had a very deliberate pattern of targets," said Holmes. "I suspect their twisted logic means they would seek to spare 'innocents'... or maybe simply reuse the device."

The rhyme was more chilling than anyone realized.

"How do you know it's not simply a clock?" asked Holmes.

"It's different," said the boy. "Clocks go tick tock. The Ticker Man goes tick tick."

"And where does the ticking come from?" Holmes asked.

"Dunno. Everywhere. Nowhere. We chase it around!" the boy said, growing visibly suspicious.

The children were perturbed by Holmes' questioning, so we entered the house and spoke to its custodian, Humphrey Ventham. Holmes told him about the erroneous package, omitting mention of the bomb.

"I started five years ago. Previous custodian was Roberta Pepys. Strange old bird. I can imagine her losing something like that, especially with no resident on the label. Just before I was hired, a lot of stuff was dumped in the sub-basement. Perhaps it's down there. Or accidentally given to a resident."

Of the current occupants, three had been here 15 years ago.

Jill Morgan was a spinster who worked as a tutor in her rooms on the ground floor. Her students had been singing the "Ticker Man" rhyme in the courtyard during their break.

"Childish nonsense," she hissed, hitting her cane on the ground. "You spend weeks teaching them literature and history, and the second you pause it's Ticker Men and Tocker Men."

"Have you heard any ticking here?" asked Holmes.

"Of course I've heard ticking!" she said, pointing her cane at a carriage clock mantelpiece. "And do not call me dear, Mr. Jones."

"No, other ticking. Not a clock, more like a device?"

She looked confused. "Never heard of ticking mice before. There's the death-watch beetle. Maybe mice nibbling might sound like ticking. Absurd."

Holmes spoke louder. "How long have you lived here?"

"Seventeen years. Inherited it from my brother Jack," she said. "Don't like the other residents, but it suffices as a place to teach. Education is crucial, don't you think? For boys and girls?"

A surprisingly modern view for a lady who seemed like a Georgian relic.

"Do you know Jonathan Horner?" asked Holmes, naming one of the other long-time residents.

She frowned. "The clockmaker? Dreadful man. Wandering the halls at all hours. Says he has insomnia. Ridiculous. What has he to worry about? He's rich, his son is prosperous. He's looking to grab someone in the dark. Perhaps he's the Tocker Man."

"What about Dr. Anthony Foster?"

"Who's an imposter??"

"DOCTOR FOSTER. Do you know him?" bellowed Holmes.

"Oh, I see. He's the only decent person here. Helped me with my problems, never charges me, so kind."

"Did either receive a package in error? Several years ago?"

"I have no idea. Such a thing does not concern me. If you don't mind, break time is over."

Jonathan Horner was an older man, and gazed at us wearily as his valet escorted us in. Holmes peered around with interest.

"Mr. Horner, if you are a clockmaker, why is there not a single clock in your house?"

"That's often the first observation most make. Truthfully, I hate clocks. They are my work, they make me money, but I won't have them in my house. My sleep is bad enough without their incessant ticking."

"Shouldn't you be at work now?" asked Holmes.

"My son has it all well in hand," said Mr. Horner. "I can go to work now, but we would have to terminate your interrogation."

He removed his eyeglasses with trembling fingers, rubbing his eyes.

"I apologize. My disposition is much affected by sleeplessness. Forty years of nightmares, 17 of them in this building."

"What is the cause?" asked Holmes.

"I had some experiences when I was younger that I find difficult to forget," said Mr. Horner. "In Crimea. War is an abomination."

Holmes asked Horner if he had heard the ticking noise.

"You mean the 'Ticker Man' from that children's song? No. I do hear the children charging around the corridors during the day. I swear that woman encourages them to do it. Why can't they run around outside?"

"Have you ever received a package not intended for you?"

Horner looked guilty. "I daresay your powers of perception would get it out of me anyway. I once received cigars meant for a Thomas Horner. I regret to say, I pretended I didn't know and smoked the lot! Is that what this is about?"

Holmes asked him about the other two suspects.

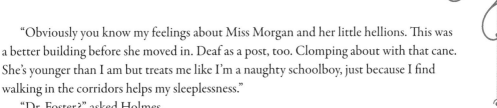

"Obviously you know my feelings about Miss Morgan and her little hellions. This was a better building before she moved in. Deaf as a post, too. Clomping about with that cane. She's younger than I am but treats me like I'm a naughty schoolboy, just because I find walking in the corridors helps my sleeplessness."

"Dr. Foster?" asked Holmes.

Mr. Horner raised a trembling teacup to his lips and took a sip.

"He is someone who I thought you would already have in your books, Mr. Holmes. He's very careful not to bring any objectionable people here, but occasionally one visits unprompted, and he has to shoo them away before anyone notices what they look like. He's not a medical doctor, he's a scientist, and I think he trades entirely with the criminal classes."

"You've seen these 'criminals?'" asked Holmes.

"As I say, I've heard them. Shouting about him selling them equipment. We're all too afraid to report it to the police, but I imagine you can do something about it."

Mr. Horner's appraisal of Dr. Foster was not incorrect. When we arrived at his rooms, he seemed to have had advance notice of our visit. He had rows of empty tables that had notable burn marks and acidic scarring, but no visible scientific equipment.

Dr. Foster himself was clearly unhappy about our visit, but he did not have the same manner as many of the underworld figures we would often encounter. He was a younger man than I expected, and seemed sad rather than hostile.

"Yes, I do have a laboratory," he said after Holmes asked after the missing equipment. "But I'm having my inventory cleaned at the moment, so I can't conduct any experiments."

"Are you permitted to perform experiments in this building?" asked Holmes. "Is there not a risk of an accident?"

"Not with my methods. I am very diligent, especially as I know children come here to have lessons," he said.

"I should say you manufacture chloroform and make things out of Indian rubber. Coshes?" said Holmes after he had peered around the room.

"How did you...? That's correct," he said carefully. "Chloroform is frequently used as an anaesthetic in medical procedures."

"Yes, but can it not also be poisonous?" said Holmes.

"Yes, but only if used in the incorrect quantities. I am very careful to instruct customers to use it only in small doses," Dr. Foster said.

"And what of the coshes?" asked Holmes. "Also an anaesthetic?"

"Well, they do induce unconsciousness," he said, smiling, then realized his joke had not amused Holmes. "Let us just say, they are preferable to a knife in the belly."

Holmes asked Dr. Foster about "The Ticker Man."

"Oh yes, brrr! That's the kind of thing that would have kept me up at night as a child. I had a terrible imagination for such nasty things. Though I note that the rhyme seems to encourage one to chase the Ticker Man. The violence is threatened by the singer. Once I learned about what real nasty things lived in the world, the creatures of my imagining seemed diminished somehow. Perhaps that's why I'm trying to improve things. But I have actually heard ticking in the house, near the basement door."

"Neither Miss Morgan nor Mr. Horner have heard that," said Holmes.

"Well, Miss Morgan's hearing is severely damaged," said Dr. Foster. "I provide her with ear drops but it's a placebo, I'm afraid. I'm not a medical doctor, but I've seen it before. I think her ear drums were damaged by being too close to some great concussive force. I don't charge her for the treatment because it's just water."

"Not because you are old friends? You went to the same school," said Holmes.

"How did you know that?" said Dr. Foster with surprise.

"That certificate on your wall; I saw the same symbol in Miss Morgan's rooms, although it was somewhat obscured," said Holmes.

"Yes. Well, we did, but she was forced to leave. No fault of mine, of course.

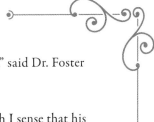

She's unaware of our connection and I'd prefer you kept it that way," said Dr. Foster peevishly.

"What about Mr. Horner?" asked Holmes.

"Well, that man is suffering from a severe lack of sleep. Although I sense that his problems stem from earlier than that. All the time I have lived here, he has had those shaking hands. What must the clocks he makes be like, I wonder? Ah, that's too cruel a thought," he said.

We left Dr. Foster and made our way to the door of the basement where, if we concentrated, we could indeed hear a strange ticking noise.

"I know two things now, Watson. None of those people received the package, and it was indeed thrown into the basement. And one of those people is the original bomber."

Question: Who does Sherlock Holmes suspect created the time-bombs?

Hints: Mr. Horner has shaky hands.
The rhyme encourages people to find the Ticker Man.
Dr. Foster's equipment leans toward non-lethality.
Miss Morgan's hearing means she can't hear ticking.

50   The Anathema Archive

"Watson!" cried Holmes, rousing me from my sleep.

He was hunched over his desk, breathing heavily. His corpse-like pallor and the manner of his breathing were alarming.

He was muttering, struggling to maintain eye contact with me, but managed to communicate.

"They poisoned me... same way as Mycroft. It was a file... they infused the pages of a police case with poison, then sent it to the Archive... it was the only way to get to him. He was defended at Whitehall and home. That story about the knights... Mycroft wrote it; it's about his past... Gutterbridge, Diddcott, Lassiter. Speak to Brendan Keoneen, trust him..."

Holmes then slumped onto the desk, unconscious, possibly comatose. I examined the desk to see if the files were there, but there were none. The rule was that any file in the Anathema Archive had to remain in the basement, and despite his leeway, Holmes had mainly stuck to that.

But I knew what he was referencing. Brendan Keoneen was Mycroft's colleague, but the other three were people who had been involved in sending files to the Archive:

- Oleander Gutterbridge, the detective doing a bad imitation of Holmes.
- Rosamond Diddcott, the incendiary flower seller with surprising acuity.
- Roderick Lassiter, the spy with the paper-thin disguise.

If what Holmes said was true, they were all former colleagues of Mycroft. And one was the poisoner.

My task, now, was to identify and catch a trained secret agent who had managed to trick and poison the two greatest minds on the planet. If I failed, they would die, and the world itself could be plunged into war.

I asked Mrs. Hudson for a glass of scotch.

Mr. Keoneen's people came and transported Holmes carefully to Mycroft's rooms, where he was laid in a bed next to his brother, so that the medical team could monitor them both. But the prognosis was not good.

I asked Mr. Keoneen about Holmes' comment.

"I suppose I must tell you. We called ourselves 'The Men of Good Intent,'" he said, ruefully. "Even though two of us were women. A project of my father, Aubrey. There was me, Mycroft, Roderick, Oleander, Rosamond, and Estelle Morgenstern. Estelle now runs the Archive as..."

"Mrs. Grabber?" I said.

"Quite so. The idea was to influence foreign policy from within England. Fake stories in newspapers, false documents on bodies. Stage events to spook or mislead visiting dignitaries or foreign agents. Subtly."

"Lassiter and Gutterbridge were subtle?" I said with disbelief. "Mrs. Diddcott?"

"They make a big show, I know. But when our group acted, it would be in the dark. We'd move silently, wearing outfits that made no sound and were hard to see. We would carry easily concealed, quiet weapons."

"Assassinations?" I asked.

"Only as a very last resort. Murder is a blunt tool. And then my father developed the Royal Blood. The ultimate poison."

"I recall, he was a famous chemist," I said.

"Indeed. The Royal Blood is undetectable by any conceivable test. The perfect murder weapon. Some of our group thought it would be an indispensable tool. Kill with impunity and no one would know."

"You disagreed?" I said.

"This kind of power is what we were fighting," said Mr. Keoneen. "Mycroft agreed, as did Estelle and my father. Rosamond, Oleander, and Roderick thought it was wrong not to use such a gift."

"The group split?" I asked.

"Almost. Father had the deciding vote, both as leader and as the formula's creator. He

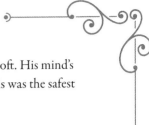

proposed to keep only half the formula, and give the other half to Mycroft. His mind's decline due to his age meant the documents were the only copy, and this was the safest thing to do. Or so we thought."

"He died. Poisoned?" I asked.

"Yes. I don't know the culprit, but I can say whoever did it does not have the whole formula. Father fell into a coma, the kind that currently affects Sherlock and Mycroft. That comes from being exposed to only half the formula. The Royal Blood is two compounds. Either induces a coma. Combined, they are undetectably deadly."

"And the cure?"

"Is to be given the same compound again. The chemistry is beyond my comprehension. But in the coma my father's body slowly failed. The same fate awaits the Holmes brothers. Do you have a plan, Dr. Watson?"

"I fear I can't find the culprit without Holmes," I said. "Sherlock, I mean."

"Yes, I understand what it's like to rely on Holmesian insight," said Keoneen with a sigh.

"Inspector Hopkins is good in a pinch, but he wants to stay with Sherlock and Mycroft to ensure there are no further attempts on their lives," I said.

"We are men of action, you and I," said Lord Keoneen. "So, here's our action: get all the culprits in one place. Then shake 'em up. But how to gather them?"

"I fear it's simple. We tell them we have the other half of the formula," I said.

That would mean our staging ground would have to be its most likely location: the Anathema Archive itself.

Estelle Morgenstern, aka "Mrs. Grabber" agreed to our plan.

"I'll do anything to help Mycroft, even if it means having those vipers in my house," she said passionately.

After several hours, all the remaining members of the Men of Good Intent stood warily in Mrs. Grabber's tiny kitchen.

Estelle Morgenstern sat warily next to Lord Keoneen, who held her hand.

Oleander Gutterbridge paced near the window, still garbed as an inadequate parody of Holmes, but with his tweed in bizarrely vibrant shades. He cradled what looked like

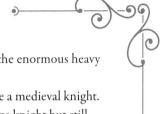

an elephant gun, which was not a Holmesian touch at all, nor were the enormous heavy army boots.

Roderick Lassiter posed against a China hutch, looking almost like a medieval knight. He was wearing brightly metallic plates, more flexible than your average knight but still cumbersome. He was cradling two loaded pistols as well.

Rosamond Diddcott, last to arrive, was dressed as if for the opera. She had a fashionable black velvet dress and a small black hat firmly pinned to her tightly bound hair with hatpins. This elegance was somewhat undermined when she removed her high-heeled boots and put her stockinged feet up on the table.

I stood by the door to the corridor, examining them all. Keoneen had suggested I might hide in the house to observe them unseen, but I felt that my presence might have more of a benefit in unsettling them.

"A reunion, is it?" Lassiter said. "I was under the impression Mycroft was still worse for wear, so I think this is less about reminiscing and more about assigning blame."

"How did Holmes find the formula?" said Mrs. Diddcott. Her accent was no longer broad cockney, instead sounding like Hertfordshire aristocracy. "I assume it was him and not either of you."

"Which Holmes?" said Mr. Gutterbridge, raising an eyebrow.

"The gentlemen you've decided to copy in every fashion," said Mrs. Grabber.

Gutterbridge's cheeks reddened. "Better than pretending to be a bent-over old washerwoman, Estelle," he snapped.

"What is the point of your charade, Oleander?" asked Mrs. Diddcott. "To irritate Mycroft? Or is it like in nature, when a weaker species imitates a predator?"

"When Sherlock 'died,' there was a space left for a man of his talent," said Gutterbridge.

"That makes you the most likely candidate to off Mycroft, I think," said Mrs. Diddcott. "Once Sherlock came back, you needed a new space to fill. And Mycroft would leave a big space."

"Actually, I rather think you're the most likely suspect, Rosamond," said Lassiter. "You hated Mycroft because unlike the rest of us, he never took you seriously as you're a woman."

"That's not why!" said Mrs. Grabber. "He respected me. He just never trusted Rosamond after she broke off their engagement."

"Personally, I think you did it, Roderick," said Gutterbridge. "You were always the most enthusiastic about the Royal Blood. If Aubrey hadn't split the formula, you'd have had us poisoning half the ambassadors in London."

"How dare you!" said Mr. Lassiter. "If we're asking who the bloodthirsty one is here, perhaps we should look to the man carrying a blunderbuss."

"I came from a hunt for this," Gutterbridge retorted. "What's your excuse for the getup and pistols?"

"How can we even be sure they have the other half of the formula?" said Mrs. Diddcott. "Watson might have the reputation of being a straight arrow, but Keoneen is a more accomplished liar than all of us combined."

She was right; we didn't have it. I was suddenly filled with concern: what if Keoneen was lying? But if Holmes trusted him and thought it was Lassiter, Gutterbridge, or Diddcott, it had to be.

"How do you know it's even the right formula?" asked Mr. Lassiter. "To the uninitiated it just looks like a bunch of letters and numbers. I suppose Sherlock could tell. Where is he, exactly?"

"Let's go down to the Archive," I said. None of them had shown any signs of guilt. They were all too skilled. Maybe going to the place where both Mycroft and Sherlock had been poisoned would provoke some reaction.

We all cautiously marched to the secret door and down into the Archive, led by Mrs. Grabber. She lit the lantern on the table and our three suspects all looked around with interest.

"This was Mycroft's little project?" said Mr. Gutterbridge. "Helping all those bobbies on the beat banish any case that got too scary for them?"

"Is this where you found the other half of the formula?" said Lassiter. "Hidden among the files? Such a mundane hiding spot. I know this place is hidden, but Mycroft's mind was always looking to provide an extra layer of obfuscation."

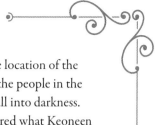

And at that moment, I suddenly realized that I did in fact know the location of the other half of the formula. I was so distracted that I didn't see which of the people in the room suddenly threw an object that smashed the lantern, plunging us all into darkness.

At that moment, I felt the incredible danger we were in. I remembered what Keoneen had said about the Men of Good Intent, how they would strike in the darkness.

And then I realized that I knew which of the suspects was the poisoner.

Question: Who does Dr. John Watson suspect is the poisoner of Mycroft and Sherlock Holmes, as well as the person who knocked out the light? And where is the formula for the Royal Blood?

Hints: All the suspects are dressed differently.
The culprit knocked out the light deliberately.
Is everyone armed?
Mycroft's story of the knights did not entirely match the story of the past.

Solutions

Solutions

Puzzle 1: The Fading Photograph

Miss Lambert, Sergeant Canning, and Katharine Aykroyd.

- Holmes felt the duke was telling the truth, so how could there be a photo of him with Lambert?
- Miss Aykroyd said she had seen them in the photo before it "faded," but Holmes' tests showed no image had been there before.
- Holmes only had the word of Canning, Aykroyd, and Lambert that there ever was an image. Remembering that Aykroyd had said scandals were not able to change careers, he realized Aykroyd and Lambert had colluded with Canning to boost her career by associating her with German royalty.
- Canning said someone forgot to seal the envelope, so Holmes realized the envelope's contents were never meant to be seen. When the blank paper slipped out, the conspirators had to pretend that the image had somehow faded before Sergeant Eldridge saw it.

Puzzle 2: The Premature Ghost

Sherlock Holmes suspects Mary Going murdered Edward Going.

While all the women had the opportunity and the motive, when they saw Edward's "ghost" it was his reflection. Therefore, the brooch appeared to be on his right side rather than his left. However, Mary said that it was "above his heart," on the left side. This suggests that she had seen him in person that night instead of merely in the reflection, and therefore was the one who killed him and took the brooch.

Solutions

Sherlock Holmes suspects Sissy Blight robbed the Larthrabores.

It made sense for all three women to have their fingerprints on the tureen, as they were all in the kitchen. But Holmes noted Sissy Blight's condition caused her to suffer excessively from the cold, and she wore gloves indoors during questioning. As it was a bitterly cold day and Sissy Blight said she was handed the tureen as soon as she entered the kitchen, she must have been wearing gloves. Her fingerprints should not have been on the tureen. She must have touched it without gloves after that, in the night (which was warmer) when she and her accomplice stole the items to fund her expensive tastes.

Mr. Patton stole the money, with an accomplice.
- Brenda Wakefield's carving skills could create a duplicate stump, but both were visible from each other.
- There's no evidence of any underground method by which the vicar might empty the bag.
- Mr. Patton had a duplicate postal worker uniform.

Had Patton stopped behind the tree to swap bags, the policeman may have noticed.

So, Patton had a confederate in uniform step out from behind the tree with the empty bag when he went behind with the full one, so they thought it was him. They swapped back when his confederate returned.

When they walked to check the bag (the pipe tobacco suggests the confederate was Arthur Mansley), he escaped while they were distracted. This explains why the vicar saw a "postman" but no policeman afterward.

Solutions

Holmes thinks Mr. Blue died by suicide, and that Mr. Blue also saved Dr. Stanners' life.

Mr. Blue's death was no accident. But neither cup contained poison.

Dr. Stanners' cup contained something unidentifiable. Holmes had no reason to disbelieve Phyllis Plum, and suspected her story was true.

Knowing both men had reason to be despairing and had met earlier in Dr. Stanners' office, Holmes suspected Blue had deliberately taken poison at Stanners' office, and that Stanners had taken poison in sympathy.

Mr. Blue then stole the antidote from Stanners' office to give to him secretly. He asked Miss Plum to add it to his friend's red cup. So, Mr. Blue died, and Dr. Stanners didn't. Dr. Stanners then covered this up.

Alexander Kingsley was responsible for the face.

Kingsley was the only witness, and Holmes was interested in Kingsley's expression. Fancher described it as "fighting the fear" but it could be a determined expression.

Consider this: did Kingsley actually want to inherit the money?

His father had rejected his grandfather's fortune and left the USA. Alexander Kingsley spent his time seeing the world and had little to do with his father's work.

His mother was determined that he inherit, but the way he idolized his father's rebellion suggested he saw a similar path for himself. Not wishing to disgrace his mother by rejecting his inheritance, he pretended to be frightened off by a ghost.

Holmes also thinks Bromwell knew his son did not want to inherit, and contrived the whole situation in order to give him an opportunity to avoid it.

Solutions

Mrs. Finch is the robber's accomplice.

Holmes noted that the clerk said both ladies put their bags down to gather up the broken scales.

Mrs. St-John's description of her bag being chased by bees suggested it was flowery, and it matched with a red hat, meaning red flowers, like poppies. Mrs. Finch's bag has poppies on.

Mrs. St-John gets confused, so she could have accidentally picked up Mrs. Finch's bag.

Mrs. Finch's hand movements were a signal to the robber that the bags were swapped, so he could get the key. Afterward, she swapped them back while everyone was stunned. Then she could use her "childhood friend" to take over the shop.

Solutions

Holmes suspects Charles Chanticleer was responsible for the disappearance, but didn't disappear.

Holmes noted that if the unfit Chanticleer had entered the box and run underneath to the back door, he would have been breathless and would take longer than ten seconds.

Chanticleer would swap with O'Malley, who wore Chanticleer's outfit. O'Malley then entered the box, dropping through the trapdoor, while Chanticleer revealed himself quickly at the back.

O'Malley suggested that he was a friend in awe of Chanticleer, but the other two suspects said the two didn't get on and argued about weight. If O'Malley doubled for Chanticleer every night, it might have played a factor whether the trapdoor worked.

So, Holmes realized that O'Malley had entered the box and, either by accident or by design, fallen through fatally into the water. Chanticleer disguised himself as his own assistant, faked his disappearance and escaped his debtors, living as O'Malley.

Holmes suspects Jacob Lassiter is the burglar.

Holmes immediately recognized that "the code" was not a real code at all.

All three suspects work in the office. Lassiter had stopped paying for his son's courses and education, yet his son was still able to attend them.

Mr. Morrison kept the accounts, Jacob said he could develop any skill given time, and had a flair for impersonation.

Solutions

So, Holmes concluded that the numbers were not a code, but a form of practice: Jacob Lassiter practising Gregory Morrison's handwriting. Holmes said the handwriting did not match one of our suspects, but two: Lassiter, then Morrison.

Jacob had been embezzling from his father as a way of funding his learning. Morrison hadn't noticed.

Jacob had to learn to copy Morrison's handwriting to write alternative books, then commit the robbery to swap them. The paper accidentally fell out and he was lucky it led them to overlook the truth.

Puzzle 10: The Forgotten Folly
Gilbert Dial was aiding Faber's captors.

None of the three connect to the kidnappers, but they can't be eliminated. One of them, however, lied.

Faber's captivity was over winter. He was cold and Ethel said the ground was hard. The Festival of Sinterklaas is in December; St. Valentine's Day, source of Ether's plight, is in February.

Gilbert Dial claimed he picked apples for his horse. But there would be no apples growing during winter.

His excuse is a lie, a cover.

Mr. Smit saw him carrying something, but that was Dial bringing Faber his food, then moving away.

Solutions

None of them blackmailed Jeremiah Crookshank.

Crookshank was a miserable miser whose reputation was enough to keep his business going, even after death.

They said he was nasty, but he never acted out his "threats."

Mary Haldon continued writing, Peter Golden vaccinated his workforce, and Josephine DeBauvau's school remained open. Because they were all blackmailing him?

No, he was secretly funding them. But they could tell no one, because his business depended on his tyrannical image.

That's why Miss Haldon commented no one knew him, and Miss DeBauvau struggled to insult him.

Holmes decided this case should remain "unsolved."

Holmes suspects Katherine Dagworthy is the poisoner.

All three had the opportunity as there's unlimited access to the kitchen for all the girls, and all three had details that suggested their involvement and motives. The simplest indicator was that Mary Catford and Millicent Smythe were reluctant to eat any food due to their fear of being poisoned, while Katherine Dagworthy, despite her apparent concern, did eat while talking to Holmes and Watson. Because she knew she couldn't be poisoned, she was the one doing the poisoning.

Solutions

Brom Brown was the robber.

Holmes felt that though the other two had motives: Mrs. Fike to finance her house, Mr. McFee to quit being an undertaker. Brown was still the most likely candidate. Even if as he said he was illiterate, he could get a friend to write the notes.

Holmes' first note was a copy of the Reaper from the original notes as a comparison to Mrs. Fike's own drawings. The style did not match.

His third note was a copy of the threatening notes' style, to see if Holmes' supposition that McFee was scared was accurate. His fear seemed genuine, so it was unlikely had he written the originals.

So, his second note was to Hopkins. He handed it to him in a way that Brown, if able to read, could do so. Holmes knocked the table and Brown flinched before Hopkins' reaction, indicating he could indeed read, and was lying to cover the fact that he had written the notes.

Cecil Moncrieff killed Horace Creaser and built him into a wall.

All the suspects had opportunity to kill him, and none of them much liked him. The key clue was the quality of the wall.

Holmes realized where the body was after seeing the article stating the wall needed reinforcement. Mr. Gunter and Mrs. Tandforth knew how to build a solid wall, but Moncrieff had much less experience and so would be more likely to build a wall that developed problems. He could have altered the plans for a space for Creaser to be sealed away without others realizing.

Solutions

Puzzle 15: The Red Right Hand 64

Luther Williams stole the compass and left the handprint.

Pattins' account and the logbook confirmed that Strong lost his hand the year before. He had no reason to leave a red handprint at the scene.

Pattins has no history of crime and no connection with Necessiter, and couldn't preserve the hand for a year in good condition without ice. Other preservation methods would shrivel it.

Strong confirmed it was his left hand of which Luther made a mould. However, Holmes noticed plaster of Paris on the rubber glove, suggesting the mould was reversed, making it a right-hand version. Williams could have created the inverse cast by accident, and also have known about Necessiter's compass, the motive for his theft.

Puzzle 16: The Character Assassin 68

Arnold Joynes is responsible, but Jason Reynolds didn't die. Because he never lived.

All accounts say how they never saw or met Reynolds, except Joynes.

Joynes stated that Reynolds had no past. People assumed Mars O'Malley disappeared after Reynolds died, but it could be before. And if he drowned, the ink would have run on the documents.

Considering all the false names in the novels, was Reynolds a false name? Jason Reynolds is in fact an anagram of Arnold S. Joynes. He wrote the books himself and put a parody of himself in them to avoid suspicion.

Joynes used his police connections to obtain the drowned body of Mars O'Malley, then shaved him, redressed him and put forged documents onto the corpse, to eliminate his dangerous pseudonym.

Solutions

Miss Montserrat planted the statue, but that's not all she did.

Holmes noticed that Thigsby stated Miss Montserrat was as beautiful as the *Venus de Milo* but "without an apple."

But the true *Venus de Milo* couldn't hold an apple, as it hasn't any arms. Meaning the exhibition *de Milo* is fake, as Holmes noticed as soon as he arrived.

Miss Montserrat seemed to have more knowledge than both men, and as an artist she could have created the object as a distraction so she could swap the *de Milo* for the forgery.

Money or revenge on the men who scorned her? Holmes would shortly find out…

Solutions

Puzzle 18: The Accidental Burglar

The "third man" was Lord Tristram Meriwether. Oscar Guildenstern did not exist.

Sergeant Kite said there had been "threats to his li…" Was he going to say life, or livelihood?

He looked like the "third man," but would he wander around with a known criminal?

Gertrude Long had no motive or connection.

Tristram Meriwether had no obvious criminal connections, but had a grudge against Jones.

Holmes thought the descriptions of "Big John" and "The Hunchback" sounded rather theatrical. So, two men wearing disguises took Jones to another location to crack a safe, then back to his house. A real crime, or a ruse?

The Elsinore Club is named after the play *Hamlet*, which has a character named Guildenstern.

Meriwether referenced *Richard III*, which features a hunchback.

The Merry Wives of Windsor features the corpulent Falstaff.

So, when Jones later saw "Big John," he wasn't wearing his false beard and belly. Meriwether ("The Hunchback") was now standing straight.

The whole thing was a prank on Jones, repaying his accusations by making him believe he was a criminal.

Solutions

Puzzle 19: The Disappearing Roofer **80**

Holmes suspects Walter Mochrie is responsible for Maynard Proops' disappearance.

He knew that Vranch wasn't lying, so Proops did fall off the roof.

Lawrence saw him fall past the window, but she was too old to have caught him.

Walter Mochrie claimed he hadn't seen him at all as he passed on the cart. But he takes his cart directly past the house, literally on the road right next to it.

So, Proops fell off the roof into the straw at the back of Mochrie's cart. The thunder and rain meant they didn't hear or see it. Then Proops bribed Mochrie to keep quiet and lie, so Proops could escape without being attacked by Stiles.

Puzzle 20: The Beastly Lair **84**

Mayor John Fairbairn was the figure in the lair.

Duncan Murray was given to exaggeration, but he probably did see something that matched his description.

Mallifer insists the fur trapper isn't a trapper at all, so the idea that they were his furs is dubious.

The mayor is 60 but with a full head of hair, and his father was bald at 25. Maybe his hair wasn't real? The mayor is said to be vain...

Now the tableau makes sense. The small pelts are wigs, and the mayor was being measured for a new hairpiece. He realized Murray had seen him, so sent a manservant to knock him out in the hope it seemed like a dream. Instead, it became a nightmare...

Solutions

Desdemona Smythe hired Mr. Threlfall.

She claimed she realized the truth about Mrs. Haskin after the fire, but the fire happened before the 11th edition of *Palimpsest*. Rooker wrote an article in the 10th edition which he said helped her realize the truth. However, she couldn't evict Haskin then.

As the flat numbers are in Roman numerals, Flat 2 is "II" and 3 "III." When Holmes found the detached "I," he realized the truth: Smythe hired Threlfall to burn Flat 2. But the dropped "I" made him think Flat III was Flat II. He torched the wrong premises...

Reverend Cooper was responsible for Harney Barlow's disappearance.

Barlow's biggest connection seemed to be with the vicar, a former mariner.

Roland Beukes said he could see that night because of the moon. But he didn't mention the lighthouse light, implying that it was off, a danger to any ships in the area. Beukes described the tower being tall and far away, but his lack of depth perception meant it could have been closer.

Holmes concluded the tower was the mast of a ship crashing into the rocks. Its "spikes" were where the booms of the ship had broken. The crashing sound was the boat against the rocks, with the tremor caused by the final impact.

Reverend Cooper said Beukes' description of the tower resembled a cross. Only an unbroken ship mast would. This suggests Cooper and Barlow were part of a smuggling ring that operated in the area and Barlow's negligence led to the boat crashing and Cooper's anger.

Solutions

"Dr. Watson" is Holmes.

All three possibilities can't be Holmes. He couldn't starve himself or grow a beard in two days, cut off limbs, and couldn't shrink to a child's size.

As Hopkins entered, "Watson" said, "I guarantee that Sherlock Holmes is in this room!" He also said Holmes was right under his nose as Watson stroked his "moustache."

He didn't rush to help Crelbourn when the real Watson would have. When Ormerod said Watson had been at the battle, he looked first to the back of the room before looking at "Watson" by the window. And when Ashwood was dancing, Hopkins heard a muffled chuckle from the back of the room: the hidden, real Dr. Watson!

Leonard Bean is the Bayswater Butcher. But not just because he is a butcher in Bayswater.

All that's known about the Butcher is that they were feared and protected because they were needed.

Slate provides important hats, and feared because of his frightening appearance and voice? Unlikely.

Lady D'August provides weapons to the underworld, but they are not in short supply, and again the butcher phrase means little.

Dr. Watson noticed several things in Leonard Bean's back room. A scalpel to cut beef. Syringes might be used by a butcher for some reason, but a stethoscope? These are the tools of a doctor.

So, Bean is obviously an underworld doctor. Hence criminals' fear of him, not wishing to go under his knife. That's why they protected him.

Solutions

Puzzle 25: The Hidden Riches 102

John Chishull committed the robbery.

Edwin North is now wealthy, but his inheritance is legitimate. Cuthbert Cook could have gambled the money away but doesn't have the skill to commit the crime, although he could just be feigning ignorance.

Chishull represented himself as a waiter who had to secure permission to speak to Holmes and Watson. Yet when he coughed from his dry throat, the maître d' placed a glass of water next to him. He quickly reversed his decision, too late. Holmes suspected Chishull was the true owner of the restaurant, opened with ill-gotten funds.

Puzzle 26: The Watch in the Well 105

Phineas Arrow was responsible for his own death, although Michael Stammers' actions contributed to it.

Arrow argued with Stammers that morning about repairs, and Stammers said, "the links were worn," implying he couldn't repair them until he got out of bed.

Perhaps the links that were worn were the watch chain, which would explain why Arrow would have to be asleep to allow him to take it and have it repaired.

Phineas Arrow went to investigate the well, and while leaning over, his watch chain snapped and his watch fell in. Arrow decided to go in but drowned. The death, "covered up" as an accident, actually was one.

Solutions

Puzzle 27: The Golden Snuffbox
Sergeant Ardron was protecting Oliver Boardman, Henry Von Trapp, and himself.

The "golden snuffbox" was empty and had gold paint on it. Holmes also noted Boardman and Von Trapp called the sergeant by his first name, despite alleging they are not close acquaintances.

The box was "dangled" in front of Miss Jankis, only for her to be immediately grabbed by the sergeant.

When Sergeant Ardron said, "well, maybe...," Miss Jankis assumed he would suggest she turn herself in, but he may have been asking for a bribe.

Holmes deduced the men ran a regular scam in this cafe, to extort any tempted thieves. When Miss Jankis almost blew it by surrendering, Ardron sent the case to the Archive to escape scrutiny.

Puzzle 28: The Impenetrable Fortress
Dr. Jakob Harket broke into the office.

The key's lack of teeth means locksmiths like Leander Loudermilk couldn't pick the lock.

The idea that the door uses cameras is a deception by Lord Stone. If it was face-activated, how could Holmes use the key?

Holmes understood how the door operated when he saw the key move closer to the metal lamp unaided, and when the metal filings on his hands clung to it. The key is magnetic. Electrical scientist Dr. Harket figured out the lock's secret and used a magnet to open it.

Solutions

Puzzle 29: The Flying Needletail 116

Liam McCracken has the key.

The train was running for 30 minutes without crashing or running out of fuel. This implies the engine room isn't empty and there's someone inside, which wouldn't suggest Hegarty's motive of destruction.

Shaver may have chosen to assassinate the ambassador, but he shows no sign of being violent or passionate, plus could have simply poisoned the tea.

There are only nine unconscious passengers in the dining car. One is missing. Iain Cleeves, the transport magnate, would know how to drive a train, taking it to a hidden location where they can steal the gold, or the innovative train itself. McCracken was absent from the luggage carriage when the tea was drugged and the time Hegarty was taken from the engine, making him the most likely candidate.

Puzzle 30: The Deadly Yardarm 120

Crispin Haversham was the last to die.

Haversham had an extra injury on his forehead.

Holmes knew Haversham's injury was consistent with being hit by the yardarm, the other injury sustained from falling backward.

The others' head injuries came from falling on the deck, not from the yardarm, but from poisoned champagne.

Haversham's weaker constitution meant that he felt driven to eliminate his rivals in an underhanded way. They fell backward, banging their heads, their glasses breaking.

Alexander had just enough life to try to carve "POISON" in the deck, but Haversham took the knife.

Solutions

Haversham would have to return to land single-handedly, and in his inexperience he got poleaxed by the yardarm. Ultimately, his family couldn't claim the money due to the murder clause.

Bob Smith is responsible for Algy Williamson's disappearance, but only because of his misunderstanding.

Fulton Sirk shouted to Bob Smith that Williamson was descending the left-hand stairs. He met Smith on the landing, assuming Smith had ascended the left-hand stairs. Smith didn't see Sirk descend and assumed he'd come down what he thought were the left-hand stairs.

There are two staircases. Smith said the light was left of the door. Watson, who is left-handed but holds his gun in his right, put his gun away to switch the lights on, meaning the switch was on the right. Smith cannot tell left from right. So, he was actually ascending the right-hand stairs, and Williamson slipped past him.

Solutions

Puzzle 32: The Willing Prisoner... 127
Benton Book willingly entered the prison.

Each of the men is lying for various reasons. But Holmes noticed that although Benton was being "taken" to Grout's cell for "punishment," he seemed to have no injuries or fear of Grout.

Why was he shaking dirt from the mail bag he was sewing? Why sew mailbags instead of breaking rocks with his strength? It points to Benton using his real skill, digging. He's making a tunnel so Grout can escape Newgate Prison. The dirt in the mailbags is from the tunnel. He used his supposed transgressions as an excuse to be "dragged" to Grout's cell.

Puzzle 33: The Uncursed Necklace.. 132
Leonard Baxter killed Peter Garton.

In the three witness accounts, there is speculation about where Peter Garton went and why. His wife and sister show distaste for him, while Leonard is very positive. What Holmes noted was that the other two accounts didn't offer ideas about his actions, while Baxter's was detailed about events that happened after Garton had left the shop.

Holmes surmised Leonard Baxter was not in fact friends with Peter Garton (both his wife and sister attested he did not really have friends), but instead Baxter was obsessed with him (following him about in the shadows). Garton caught him and rebuffed him, and in the ensuing fight Baxter accidentally killed him.

Solutions

Puzzle 34: The Misplaced Cadaver
Roger Turvey is responsible for the appearance of the clothed body at the dig.

Simeon Belgeddes likes to give the air of being a "vampire," and a body being found at the dig would help reinforce this illusion.

Miss Divola disliked Gerald Simkins, but there is no evidence she would kill him.

Holmes deduced the body was in fact a Saxon corpse from the dig that had been dressed in modern clothes. Turvey was smuggling bodies out of the dig disguised in coffins, to send abroad and sell as the bodies (or body parts) of saints, a process overseen by Gerald Simkins.

As they transported one, the cart hit a rut and the body tumbled out, the wooden splinters on the body coming from the box in which it was hidden.

Puzzle 35: The Perplexing Puzzle
Hamish Roper killed the architect and stole the cup.

Who was able to see the light through the window at sunset? Mrs. Dunwiddy owned the house, so could have seen it. Mr. Unstible was permitted on the grounds in the morning, and was able to enter the house.

Mr. Roper was seen by Dunwiddy at the station when she had to catch the 4 o'clock train. Roper's fingers were frozen from winter cold, suggesting the sun sets around 4–5 pm. The maze took two hours, and the lock would open after 51 minutes. This meant he'd be inside the house at 6:51 pm at the earliest, so it must have been dark when he was inside, and he couldn't have seen it.

Solutions

Puzzle 36: The Five Cherubs 142

Athens Wilson threw the plaster cherubs through the windows.

The only money was stolen was from Smithson's safe, so this must be the real target. The safe was opened by someone who knew the code. Smithson says only he knew it, but he had written it down. Athens Wilson visited Smithson's before the robbery, so must have found the paper with the code.

Wilson cannot be seen to associate with criminals, so he couldn't just pass the combination along. Instead, he decided to signal his contact; by using his own cherubs, he could be sure they would know it was him. He targeted restaurants whose door numbers revealed the code: 12, 101, 8, 89. Also, by targeting restaurants he hoped to hide the real target, making it look just part of a pattern of burglaries.

Holmes wasn't certain 12101889 was the code, but he did ascertain that Smithson's restaurant started there on the 12th of October 1889.

Puzzle 37: The Angel's Share 146

Liam Flanagan is keeping Mary Flanagan captive.

Holmes realized the "8" was not an "8" at all. Mary, a mathematician, was using a mathematical symbol ∞, the symbol for infinity, to signal that she was at the bottom of the "bottomless" well. Her father is the only person with access and stores his rarer bottles down there. She took one of those bottles and made the symbol, hoping someone would find it and work out where she was. Flanagan hoped that he could force her to marry Patrick Fricker and seal his alliance.

Solutions

Rex Heard attacked Bernard Green.

It is true that all the alibis are uncorroborated, and self-serving. There's an element of fiction to each of them, even if Gutterbridge doesn't see it.

But Rex Heard's alibi is particularly fictional. Holmes noted that all the aspects of it related directly to objects in Gutterbridge's Holmesian office:

- Gave Bill Piper the slip—Pipe tobacco in slipper.
- Slipped on oil, knocking lights out—Kerosene lamp.
- Tied up in paper mill, drowning in ink, saved with turpentine—Blotter with ink and chemicals.
- Knife to cut bonds, thinking Piper would follow him to the "ends of the earth"— Globe nicked with knife cuts.
- Knock the stuffing out of him—Chair losing stuffing.
- Problems made bigger—Magnifying glass.

This explains why Heard was looking around Gutterbridge's office so intensely.

Solutions

Sigmund DeVries is responsible for the death of Sir Hugh Brown.

When Mr. Finch left, Sir Hugh told him the chimneys would be clean. Sir Hugh had hired Mr. DeVries to clean them, refusing to pay until he did it. DeVries said that should he create such a machine, the suction would be so intense as to suck large objects into the flue.

Holmes realized DeVries had managed to do so, and that the hole in the attic was an attachment for the nozzle of the vacuum cleaner. He'd taken it into the attic and connected it to demonstrate to Sir Hugh. The immense vacuum pressure combined with the sealed room sucked him into the chimney, where he suffocated. DeVries, horrified, then left the building and pretended he hadn't been there.

Noah Perceval stole the staff.

As he didn't care about the dukedom, stealing the staff would benefit him: there would be no title for his brother to envy, removing the danger to his life. He could frame his sister, as then there was no way she would face vengeful repercussions from Parker. Alcesta may have sensed this, accusing him on her effigy.

Holmes noted that the stone of the shield was newer, cleaner than the rest of the effigy. It was a more recent addition, when Thomas had decided to open the house and crypt to visitors and wanted to hide something: his father's confession.

Once the shield was removed, Holmes saw that underneath Noah's effigy was the staff, admitting his wrongdoing.

Solutions

Isaac Williams has been attacking Mrs. Diddcott's customers.

Her brother Billy is trying to mark himself as "The Rose," but if he intends to be a fighter, attacking people anonymously won't gain him notoriety.

Nerys Bumble seems hostile, but it's more likely she's imitating Diddcott's style to ape her success.

Williams seems innocuous, but has a history of violence. He has feelings for Mrs. Diddcott, blaming the conflict on the customers, saying she needs protection.

Williams is attacking customers who he thinks upset her, leaving a red rose as, in a twisted way, a romantic gesture.

Mr. Kelley vandalized Mr. Gossamer's house.

The key is the large collars and meat, the ashen interior, Mr. Kelley's assertion that he had saved the zoo, and the men with a crate seen by Miss Barrington.

Holmes realized that the cat was not a black cat, but a baby leopard (perhaps the luck he spoke of creating was in fact due to criminal activity such as illegal animal trading). It was black due to ashes on its fur.

When Mr. Gossamer saw it, Kelley was concerned it would be discovered, so decided to try and intimidate him, smashing the windows and daubing soot on the walls to give him the impression it was related to witchcraft, framing Miss Barrington. This explains why his fights with his wife seemed related to an unseen "baby."

Solutions

Galahad killed Merlin.

It's not possible to say from the character's words or actions which of them used the Anti-Grail.

However, the guilty knight is revealed by how the author describes the characters.

Leading up to the murder, Lancelot the Bold, Galahad the Pure, and Agravain the Proud are all referred to with their descriptive suffixes. But after the murder, while Lancelot is still the Bold, and Agravain still the Proud, Galahad is no longer The Pure. As King Arthur said, the Anti-Grail is not an artefact of purity.

Mrs. Hallett put the betting slip into the hat.

The betting slip was noticeable inside the hat band. When Inspector Hallett received his hat back from George Steptoe, he would have noticed it, but he didn't.

He stopped for a funeral procession, and it's traditional to remove your hat as a sign of respect.

Therefore, the slip couldn't have been in the hat when he left the shop. The only culprit can be his wife, putting it in the hat after he handed it to her.

She seemed disappointed that he didn't redeem the winning slip, so Holmes suspected she had won it at Aintree, as there were no witnesses to whether she was at home, but she hadn't been able to collect her winnings.

Solutions

Eustace Raynott killed the three men.

Coppice's disinterest in the men is feigned, and he clearly has some resentment.

Isobel Meek had both the opportunity and the means as a cleaner, and knows about poison. She also has motive, due to her family's long-standing grudge against the college.

Raynott resents his position as a librarian and would rather be a lecturer. He claims not to have met them, but the other two suspects say that the three men had visited his library. Holmes suspects that Raynott might have been the source of the knowledge they used to seem intelligent, grooming them and training their abilities, only to be unacknowledged or rejected.

Holmes noted that Raynott's library was neat, with no gaps, yet he was placing a book on French mythology into a space. Holmes suspects each time the dolly was found, the man would come to Raynott and he would offer them a book about folk tales, the pages of the book impregnated with a maddening poison!

Solutions

Puzzle 46: The Invisible Knight
Victoria Chesham killed Montgomery Hoggett.

The angle of the sword's thrust suggests a tall man like Hawkwood or Vandemeer stabbed Hoggett. Either of them could have bribed or convinced their acquaintances to provide an alibi. But there wasn't enough room for two men in the passageway, let alone one to strike the blow while Hoggett stood facing the wall reading the message. And there was no accessway.

Holmes realized the belltower's shadow falling over the passageway meant you could see it from there. He noted that the sword had strange elements, like a handguard with sharp, fin-like protrusions and a cross carved into the pommel.

When he heard about Miss Chesham's skill with archery, particularly the crossbow, he deduced the truth. She had acquired the sword from the broken statue and adapted it to be fired from a crossbow. She carved the message into the passageway which was within range of the belltower. When he arrived to examine the message, she went up to the tower to provide herself with the bell-ringing alibi and fired the sword down into his stomach. This explains why Vandemeer thought the bells paused, and why there was no evidence of footprints.

Solutions

Puzzle 47: The Broken Mask
Humility McManus is the burglar.

Bright was already guilty of theft, but the crimes were 13 years previously. Why would he leave pieces of the death mask at the scenes of his crimes, knowing they could lead back to him?

Gilbert deals in stolen goods, so the robberies could have been done on his behalf, or he could be pretending to be an invalid.

The only reason the pieces would be in the people's houses were: (a) if they had bought them; (b) an accident; or (c) as a message of some kind.

Mrs. McManus' name, Humility, is a Quaker virtue name, like Praise-God Darby, and she uses the word "thee." Bright said that Praise-God's family distanced themselves and changed their name, so it's possible that Mrs. McManus was in fact related to Praise-God. She also had a hemp bracelet she fiddled with. She claimed she had never seen Praise-God, then said she wept from self-pity that she wouldn't see him "again."

Holmes realized the truth: Bright had sold Gilbert the death mask and the rope he'd used to hang Praise-God. This rope had been split up and sold to the five people. Mrs. McManus, formerly Humility Darby, had visited Gilbert and threatened him, taking the mask before tracking down and visiting the people who had the rope, stealing it back and leaving them a piece of the mask as a warning or judgement, to look upon the face of her brother.

Solutions

"Hollis Fairmane" stole the fan.

Because Lestrade suspects that Hollis Fairmane was Sherlock Holmes.

Lady Merriweather had a strange attitude toward the fan, desperate to get it back, and she was connected to shady gentlemen.

Then there is the "coal man," Hollis Fairmane, only apparently employed by Lady Merriweather and Holmes, who left coal sacks in the corridor but no mark on the carpet.

Inspector Lestrade concluded that Lady Merriweather was an agent for some outside party stationed in England. Holmes had got wind of this and, disguised as Hollis Fairmane, had got the job as coal man and then used the weighted sacks to knock a small hole in the side of the house, changing out of his dirty clothes so that he could steal the fan, which contained secret codes—the interesting markings.

Holmes must have been acting on behalf of the government, so when Lestrade spotted the fan, Holmes made up the story about Mrs. Hudson, not suspecting Lestrade would then believe his housekeeper was guilty of theft. When Lestrade finally came to him about it, he released the fan, using the opportunity to catch Lady Merriweather with her co-conspirators.

Solutions

Jill Morgan created the time-bombs.

Jonathan Horner, a clockmaker, would have knowledge of the mechanics to build a time-bomb. However, because he's on edge, his shaking hands suggest he couldn't build the bomb.

Dr. Foster has criminal connections, supplying them with chloroform and coshes. But his equipment focuses on making things less violent than bombs, providing criminals with non-lethal weapons.

Jill Morgan, the tutor, implies she has lived at the house since the time of the package being sent there. But Jonathan Horner says the place was nicer "before she came." He's lived there for 14 years, so she must have arrived after the package.

Her deafness has rendered her unable to hear the ticking. But her children hear it and roam the halls, apparently at her encouragement. This is the purpose of the "Ticker Man" rhyme, and why it encourages children to chase the ticks.

How did she lose her hearing? Dr. Foster says it was from being too close to a concussive force. Like a bomb. Possibly from testing.

Holmes concludes that Miss Morgan built and mailed the bombs out of revenge for her rejection (her pointed comment that education is vital for both genders revealing the reason she left schooling). She accidentally sent one to the building. She moved in, but unable to hear the ticking, she became a tutor so she could use the children to find it.

Solutions

I realized that Rosamond Diddcott was the poisoner of Mycroft and Sherlock Holmes, and
the one who knocked out the light.

All of the former members of the Men of Good Intent had motive to commit the
crime, both with personal animosity toward Mycroft and Sherlock, and the desire to get
the formula. They are all skilled liars and manipulators, so I knew I could not deduce the
guilty party from their words.

But I remembered what Keoneen had said about how they acted. In the dark, moving
silently, wearing outfits that made no sound and were hard to see, carrying easily concealed,
quiet weapons. And when the culprit knocked out the lights, I remembered what each of
the suspects was wearing.

Oleander Gutterbridge was wearing bright clothes and big boots and carrying an
enormous blunderbuss. Far from suitable attire and equipment for fighting in the dark.

Roderick Lassiter's outfit was if anything even less suitable, glittering, cumbersome,
loud, and with two pistols that would be ineffective in close quarters.

But Rosamond Diddcott was wearing all black. Black dress, black hat. All in quiet
fabrics. She had removed her shoes. And while she had no visible weapons, her hair was
fixed with hatpins, which I knew could often be used as stabbing weapons by women.
Especially dangerous if tipped with Royal Blood.

So, I pulled out my own secret chemical compound, a Bengal fire candle, which when
activated provided instant pyrotechnic illumination. In the dazzling blue light, I saw
Diddcott just about to strike, and I tackled her just before she could stab Keoneen with her
poisoned hatpin.

Solutions

Rosamond Diddcott refused to talk after this point. But when we searched her residence, we found half of the Royal Blood's formula, disguised as an inventory of flowers. Once they had administered it to Sherlock and Mycroft, the group members collectively decided to burn it.

Mycroft thanked Sherlock and I for our work, but refused to apologize for the Archive. "Where there is light, there must be darkness," he said. After all I had witnessed, I wasn't sure if I agreed.

But I understood what he meant about some secrecy being necessary. After all, I didn't reveal that I knew where the other half of the formula was: hidden in the words of his story about Camelot and the Anti-Grail. A perfect place of concealment for letters and numbers. Had Holmes realized this too? Probably. But remarkably, to this day we have never discussed it.

Picture Credits